Love

Debbie xx

DEBBIE TRAVIS *and*
DESIGN YOUR NEXT CHAPTER

"One of the most difficult things humans face in their lifetimes, and sometimes more than once, goes something like this: *What do I do now? How do I find my new purpose? What really makes me happy?* Debbie Travis' new book, *Design Your Next Chapter*, is the perfect literary companion to help you take the first step to actualizing your passions. Right from the opening paragraphs, you get a real sense that Debbie's experiences, both good and bad, will shine a light on taking chances and understanding that you, too, can take a leap towards new adventures in your own life. This book is not only inspiring but very funny, whimsical and infectious, and I know it will light a fire and motivate you to embrace the best things in life!"

JANN ARDEN, singer-songwriter,
and author of *Feeding My Mother* and *Falling Backwards*

"In *Design Your Next Chapter*, Debbie shares her courage, strength, beauty, confidence, experience and heart. I want nothing else in my own life than to surround myself with positive and inspiring people like this incredible woman. How wonderful that in her book she's offering us real ways to create a future for ourselves that is exactly as we dreamed it could be."

LYNN CRAWFORD, chef and cookbook author

"Honesty, passion and humour—these are the words I would use to describe my dear friend Debbie Travis. She pours her heart and soul into everything she does. This book exemplifies exactly that. *Design Your Next Chapter* takes you on a personal journey, in which you'll discover your own destination just as Debbie discovered hers. You will laugh and you will cry. And if you are searching for that missing piece of yourself, her book will throw you a lifeline."

MARILYN DENIS, television and radio host

"Debbie Travis combines her business, design and life experience in the most enjoyable, practical and stylish self-help book you'll read this year."

TRISH HALPIN, editor-in-chief, *Marie-Claire*

"Engaging and inspiring from start to finish, *Design Your Next Chapter* is a powerful reminder that when we have the courage to speak our truths and step fully into our dreams we can find the motivation to live our best lives. Diving into Debbie's new book is like spending a day with a really inspiring friend."

CATHY LOBLAW, CEO, Ronald McDonald House Charities Canada

"Let Debbie Travis be your guide, guru or best friend. She knows how to live life to the brim. In these pages, she shares both her secrets and practical steps leading to her formidable and inspiring successes. This funny, touching and smart book will surely propel readers to make startling changes in their lives."

FRANCES MAYES, author of *Under the Tuscan Sun*

"I loved it. *Design Your Next Chapter* is wonderful in its honesty, freshness, self-irony and vital spirit."

PATRICIA REINMANN, publisher, DTV

"I laughed, cried, nodded my head in agreement and had countless 'Aha!' moments. The honesty with which Debbie shares her personal journey is the magic of *Design Your Next Chapter*—a must-read for anyone looking for something more to life and having trouble turning the page. Through story-telling, humour, practical suggestions and encouragement, Debbie's book provides both the proof that monumental change for the better is possible and the guidance to make it happen."

STEPHANIA VARALLI, Co-CEO, Women of Influence

DESIGN
Your
NEXT
CHAPTER

DESIGN *Your* NEXT CHAPTER

HOW TO REALIZE YOUR DREAMS
AND REINVENT YOUR LIFE

DEBBIE TRAVIS

RANDOM HOUSE CANADA

PUBLISHED BY RANDOM HOUSE CANADA

Copyright © 2018 Debbie Travis

www.penguinrandomhouse.ca

Library and Archives Canada Cataloguing in Publication

Travis, Debbie, 1960–, author
Design your next chapter : how to realize your dreams and reinvent your life / Debbie Travis.

Issued in print and electronic formats.
ISBN 978-0-7352-7476-1
eBook ISBN 978-0-7352-7477-8

1. Self-actualization (Psychology). 2. Motivation (Psychology). 3. Success. I. Title.

BF637.S4T73 2018   158   C2018-902693-6
C2018-902694-4

Book design by Lisa Jager

Interior art: (Moroccan pattern) © ColorJuli / Shutterstock.com; (damask pattern) courtesy of the author

Printed and bound in the United States of America

10 9 8 7 6 5 4 3 2 1

TO MY BOYS, HANS, JOSH AND MAX,
AND TO ALL THOSE WHO HAVE DREAMED IT,
DONE IT, AND LIVED IT. ESPECIALLY TO THOSE
WHO ARE PRESENTLY AT LIFE'S CROSSROADS
HOPING TO TAKE THE NEXT STEP.

TABLE OF CONTENTS

Hello! 1

Dream It

Do It

Live It

PLEASE WRITE IN THIS BOOK

Just telling you this in case you think you shouldn't!

This is your handbook, both practical and personal. Fill in the blanks, tick the boxes, circle the words and write the truth to yourself (I've included a little section at the end specifically for that!). Put the book away for a while and absorb the ideas. Allow them to work on you. When you pick it up again, look to see what's changed inside you, and in your life.

HELLO!

Montefollonico, Tuscany. 2 p.m.

For the first time that day it was quiet. No hammering, no shouting, no growl of cement trucks lumbering down the steep, gravel drive. Several workers were snoozing under the olive trees. Another was propped against the wheel of his massive digger, muttering in his sleep. The plumber was napping under the picnic table, peaceful as a newborn, wrapped in the red-and-white-checkered tablecloth. Even the chickens up the hill were having a siesta, numbed into silence by the midday heat of this Tuscan summer day.

I stood very still and took in the view. It was far from finished, but I could see it at last: my dream made real all around me. It was happening.

I hope you haven't picked up this book looking for decorating tips. Don't get me wrong, I still love making the world beautiful through great design, but the journey I've been on for the last few years has been about something very different.

Many of us reach a pivotal moment when we realize that there must be more to life than our daily routine. I had one of those moments. The temptation can be to ignore it and carry on—there are plenty of reasons why our lives are the way they are—but what happens if we have the courage to come to a full stop, take a look around us and decide to journey down a completely new path? That's what this book is about.

I arrived at my own turning point a few years ago, where I had to decide whether to keep on with what I was already doing—producing my television shows and everything that went with it—or make a radical turn.

I turned. I dared to dream about an exciting next chapter and then I worked like crazy to make it happen. I am now living that dream: running a retreat I built in Tuscany for like-minded women as burned-out and in need of a change as I was. Along the way I have encountered many women (and a few men, too) in the same place I used to be, who were hungry for tools, ideas and the courage to switch careers, create their own next chapters and seek out a new life.

In these pages I'm sharing the lessons I've learned on this road—along with the fascinating and uplifting stories others have shared with me either during the daily forums (with wine!) we hold at my retreats or on my travels—to help anyone who has ever imagined wandering down an alternative road. This is a book for people who are asking "What comes next for me?" For people who have longed to make a significant change in their lives, but felt they lacked the tools to do it. For anyone who has ever wondered what it would be like to actually live their dream, who has asked, "What if . . . ?"

The women who come to my retreats in Tuscany have already done a thing or two. They might be in a job that was thrilling twenty years ago but no longer excites them. Or they are mothers whose children have moved on to their own adventures, leaving a gaping hole behind. Others come to my retreats who have achieved the goal they set for themselves, yet find that something is missing now they've finally reached the top. Women turn up who are searching for a role that is not so much about pleasing others or making money as about igniting their passion for living once again. Some have been longing to abandon the security of a salary to take a creative risk; others find that they don't care anymore about their status in the world, but want to do something that has meaning for them. Others thought they would love early retirement, but are now climbing the walls, longing for a challenge.

And then there are people like me, who still love what they are doing, but who crave less social isolation and more real social interaction.

That's one thing I learned at my own crossroads. Just keeping on going through the motions is not for me—or for anyone who wants to feel truly alive.

I can't remember life without work. When I was eleven, my day began a few hours before the school bell rang. I was a lucky girl, I thought, because I had a job. Before the rest of my family were awake, I would drag myself to the newsagent shop run by Mr. Singh, a kind and fatherly person who seemed quite exotic in the rural town in Northern England where I grew up. The shop was pungent with spices, and Indian music tantalized my ears, all of it a far cry from the kitchen at home. Rain or shine, I plonked that heavy newspaper sack over my bicycle handlebars and went door to door delivering the morning paper. Then I went to school. Every Sunday Mr. Singh rewarded me with a handful of change. I flushed with pride each time because this was my money. I had earned it.

Jump forward several decades. Luckily I'd moved up from being a paper girl, and found a calling that took me way beyond the satisfaction of earning my own money. I had begun with dabbing paint on the walls of my home in Montreal and been successful beyond my wildest dreams.

I had just wrapped up a gruelling schedule of filming my fourth television series, *All for One,* at the same time as I was running a branded product line at Canada's largest retailer, and I was exhausted. I decided to treat myself to a week of rest and recuperation, far from home and all its demands, on the tropical island of Koh

Samui, off the coast of Thailand. (I know how lucky I was to be able to take such a break.)

On my last day there, I decided to have a sauna. It was one of the new infrared things, a super-heated wooden crate with a bench inside and a slatted grate through which I could look out into the jungle. The Thai therapist had left me to steam out my bodily toxins for half an hour—and I was only eight minutes in and deathly bored with my own company. She'd told me it was okay to go outside to drink some water if I became too hot, so I felt I had permission to get out of there for a minute or two. Distraction—I desperately needed distraction!

Alongside the water bottles in the lounging area was a pile of gossip magazines, and one lonesome book. I had read just about every fact about Kim Kardashian's bottom and Justin Bieber's latest antics on the long flight over, so I grabbed the book and headed back into the oven.

The sweat-wrinkled paperback was about finding happiness. I groaned. I'd always been too busy for self-help books, or maybe I had to be so much in control of my own destiny that I couldn't acknowledge I was ever in need of the kind of help they provide. But at that moment either I kept listening to my own noisy thoughts or I opened the book. I opened the book.

The first sentence asked me to think of the things in my life that bring me happiness. Okay, that I could do. I was in my early fifties and feeling pretty good about myself. Two wonderful kids, a husband I loved and a career I'd excelled in. On top of all that, I had many friends dotted around the world and I was in good health. I figured I was high up there on the happiness spectrum.

But by the time I stepped out of the sweatbox twenty minutes later, I was beet red—partly thanks to the heat but also because I had cried so much my puffy face resembled a blow-fish. The serene and unflappable Thai therapist looked startled by the state I was in and explained to me that the mixture of the detoxing heat and the small space could make people *mindful*. That was one word for it! I wish she'd told me that before I entered that little coffin.

The book had asked one simple question: Was I happy? It rocked me to the core. The thought that I might not actually be as happy as all my many blessings should make me tore me apart. What was my problem? I really did have it all, didn't I?

On what felt like an endless flight home, I was marooned with my questions. Why was I so upset? Why did I feel traumatized by my own thoughts? What had brought on this unsettling feeling that all was not as it should be? I was tired, very tired, but surely that was understandable with everything I had going on. Much irritated me and my fuse was short because I was stressed, right?

But in the sauna, I'd realized that what made me truly happy were just three things: being with my children, being with my priceless friends, and being with my beloved husband. On the plane home, I had to admit that I was not spending enough time with these precious people.

My children were embarking on their own journeys, and that was fine—I was thrilled for them. But because I was just so busy, I did not see much of my friends, who meant the world to me—I hadn't understood how much I missed them. We spoke on all kinds of social media from Facebook to texting, Skype to WhatsApp, but rarely had face-to-face, eye-to-eye contact.

My friend Helen and I had a monthly date for a phone chat where we each poured ourselves a glass of wine and spilled our hearts out, but we were usually hundreds of miles apart. It was just not the same as sitting together on the couch on a Friday night.

What rattled me the most was that my dear husband, Hans, and I saw each other all the time as we ran our television company together, but I wasn't sure whether we were really "seeing" each other anymore.

We had met and married after a few whirlwind weeks of courtship, and then immediately had our children, one after the other. Our production business took off parallel to my initial success on television with my first show, *The Painted House*, followed by my subsequent series, and then we developed and produced a variety of other hosts' shows across the US and Canada. My life was a juggernaut of hard work, travel and endless meetings. The two of us juggled like pros: took turns shopping, cooking, picking up kids, tackling homework, travelling—negotiating the usual demands of life in a busy family. I still adored Hans more than any other human being on the planet, so why wasn't I spending more real time with him, time where we weren't working or trading chores?

Tears streamed again on the plane, distress oozing from every pore. (The wine was not helping!)

As luck would have it, I was seated next to a golden-robed Thai monk who spoke perfect English and asked me if he could help. The poor man should never have offered. After listening to an hour of me pouring out my heart, he said, "May I interject? You are wise because you are answering your own questions. The decision is there in front of you. It is very simple. Spend more time with those you love."

"But how do I do that? I am just so busy!" I wailed.

"Then don't be so busy," he said. "Change your priorities, change your attitude—focus on what makes you happy before you run out of time."

And with that he turned away from me and went to sleep.

I felt calmer for the rest of the flight home. For the next few months, I could think of little else but his advice about what I needed to do with my time—I needed to focus on being with the people who made me completely happy. My friends and family and, most of all, my old man. But how did I get off the endless wheel of work and do that? We used to live in a world where we had time off, "spare" time. There used to be a thing called a weekend, but now, thanks to technology, we never really leave the office. Mine stalked me wherever I hid.

The wonderful Italian word *basta*—so satisfying to say—means "enough." That is how I felt. *Basta!* Enough of the endless filming, the racing through airports, the collapsing exhausted every single night. I knew how to do my job inside out and upside down. I lived and breathed the television industry and I delighted in all aspects of design. I still got goosebumps when I was faced with an empty room to remake; the highlight of any day was the chance to brainstorm around a boardroom with my brilliantly talented peers. But I was tired of the push and shove of my daily work life and tired of the fact that only crumbs of time were left over for any sort of "me" life. I couldn't ignore it any longer. It was time for a new chapter.

I hope this book will help you design yours.

WHAT ABOUT ME?

The GPS was not making any sense and the over-sized map was now a crumpled ball of frustration on the back seat of the rental car. We were lost. My husband was grumpy and I was frazzled. Hans made another turn and we bumped our way down another white gravel Tuscan lane that glared back at us in the midday sun. We were trying to find our way to a small, rural bed and breakfast where we would spend a few rare days alone together.

Around the next corner, a stooped old man was ambling along minding his own business. We stopped, I jumped out, unravelled the map and showed him the place we were desperate to find. His face lit up and to our astonishment he climbed right into the back of the car. "*Avanti,*" he shouted, thrusting his walking stick between the seats, and we set off, following his emphatic instructions.

Ten minutes later, we found ourselves in a rustic farm kitchen surrounded by the old man and his family. The table was piled with steaming dishes of delicious food and jugs of red wine, and children were everywhere. Amongst the Italian chatter, of which we understood little, a young woman introduced herself in English. "I am Marissa and this is my family and our farm," she said. "I am sorry but my grandfather loves to pick up strangers, especially at lunchtime. Please stay for *pranzo*. He would like that."

And so we stayed for *pranzo* (Italian for lunch). Before the meal ended, a gaggle of neighbours dropped by. Some of them joined us for coffee, and some made a feast of the leftovers. I wondered aloud to my husband if we had fallen upon a celebration of some sort. Marissa overheard me and told me that no, this was normal, it was always like this—Italians were a sociable people. That I did not doubt. I also thought that their sociability must be really good for them: the crowd looked happy, healthy and madly alive—including the five animated octogenarians among us.

Three hours later we were back in the car with clear instructions on how to find our B & B. As we drove away, we could not stop grinning. What had just happened? That gathering had all the noise and energy of the parties I used to go to in my twenties. No wonder the Italians needed an afternoon siesta.

Two weeks later, I was back at work. The board-room at the television network always smelled of stale coffee. As the discussions droned on, my mind wandered back to that farmhouse kitchen. Everything about the experience had excited me. The family's kindness and generosity had been overwhelming. They had welcomed us, fed us and sent us on our way with arms full of their homemade goodies. They hadn't been rushing anywhere. They hadn't said, No, I can't, I'm too busy. On the plane back from Thailand, I'd realized that I really did need to change my life. No more driving myself into the ground. I needed time to reconnect with my husband, my family and friends in a serious and sustained way. Now this simple Italian experience lit up in my head like a beacon.

Was Italy where I'd find my next chapter?

The spooky thing was that as soon as I'd admitted to my daily turmoil of discontent, I saw similar signs of distress and longing everywhere. It's like after you buy a new car—suddenly you notice the same model all over the place. "Look, he's got one just like me, only in red. Hmnn, I like it in red."

I was like a moth to the flame of change, drawn to stories of how others had transformed their lives after hitting adversity or burn-out or just plain boredom. Each was like a spur, prodding me on.

At my retreats I have now met hundreds of people of a variety of ages and from all walks of life whose heads are in a similar place as mine used to be when they arrive for a week at my villa.

Some are about to become empty nesters; their sadness is palpable. I remember the way one single mother put it: "I have a year left before my last one leaves home and the loneliness is already too much. I know it's dramatic, but it's like I have a black hole growing in my heart. My daughters have been my entire life for eighteen years. I am intensely happy for their futures but I cry for myself."

Many have reached the point where they are just bone-tired with the daily commute and the same old routine. They are fed up with a work culture where being overloaded is the norm and being way too busy is *the* measure of success. Committing to a week in which they are able to step out of those roles lets one little question come to the surface: "What about me?"

Then there are those who have climbed the employment ladder successfully, but now that they are perched at the top, they have begun to sway. "I was happy during the climb but the summit has left me wanting something different. What do I do now?" Or "I'm at the top of my profession but each day has begun to feel like a carbon copy of the day before." There is nothing more deadening to the spirit than feeling like you have nothing left to learn.

Men are not immune to these same regrets and questions about whether what they're doing has any meaning, either. My brother is only forty-seven, hand-some, lively and always young to me. He was the CEO of a major ad agency in New York but, around his office, he was known as the "old man." He found it disconcerting when his young colleagues assumed they needed to explain a business concept to him. "It's as if experience today means nothing," he told me. "It just got tiring." (He quit: more about that later.)

Life can be a series of blind curves, but there can be even wilder turns as we get older. I have heard the stories of women, unexpectedly and prematurely widowed, whose melancholy wraps them in a blanket of fear for their future. I also can't count the number of women at the retreats who are dealing with the end of their marriage. One of them told me, "After the anger and tears I feel dead inside, dull and old." This past summer I heard the cruellest story from one of our guests. "I woke up one morning next to my husband of twenty-eight years and he was staring at me," she said. "Then he announced that I was past my expiry date and walked out for good." I will never forget the way all the women in the group gasped in horrified sympathy when she said this.

So many women are troubled by less dramatic issues: lives that are full of obligation but lack joy. As one announced, after several glasses of Prosecco, "I feel like the passion for life I once had has gradually dripped away, like water from a leaky faucet. I try to tell myself that I don't care, but I do care."

KINDNESS ON A PLATE

DAVID KIRKWOOD

David Kirkwood had a successful career as a broadcast executive at a major television network in Toronto. He was passionate about the job, but after several decades, realized he found little to like about the day-to-day routine. But he was okay with that because he had found a new love—tilling. Yes, literally digging in the dirt and turning over the soil. "There is nothing like it," he told me.

David and his wife, Sarah, bought a one-hundred-acre organic farm in Prince Edward County, about two and a half hours down the road from Toronto, and on weekends and holidays David threw himself into farming and, in particular, learning everything he could about how to create and sustain healthy, biologically balanced soil. This fed his soul, and so, he found, did cooking—especially when the vegetables came from his own soil.

Eventually he decided that he needed to quit his job of twenty-eight years and dedicate his next chapter to his love of food and farming; Sarah was fully supportive, even though she kept straddling their two worlds, hanging on to her job in the city. David soon realized he wasn't really capable of taking on a farming operation all by himself, so he utilized his former sales skills to approach others to get involved. He sectioned off areas so people could grow their own crops for commercial or private use, charging a nominal rent that would cover his taxes and equipment. "I could do this because I no longer need to work for a salary," he said. "I am not super-wealthy, but I have enough to live the life Sarah and I have dreamed of."

David adores farming, even the weeding: "Oh, the joy of working along a patch pulling out weeds and then looking back to see how much happier the plants are. It is my meditation practice." He soon decided to marry all the fresh organic produce he was growing with his lifelong passion for cooking to find more ways to share his good fortune with others. He'd noticed the lonely lives of single men around the county, some of them elderly, some just poor and on their own, and often without much of a clue about how to eat healthily or cook for themselves. He decided to hold cooking classes for groups of these men where they would work through making each dish on a menu, then savour the delights of a meal together.

It's been a resounding and deeply satisfying success. "At first these guys were pretty silent," David said. "Now they chat away about nutrition, food, recipes and of course their lives. The talk is always positive. Some of them just didn't know how to cook because no one ever taught them. Many are lonely."

David used his next chapter to draw people together over the love of good food.

Sometimes what troubles them is as simple as this: "I'm bored—bored with my life." With so many wonders in the world, I think we are almost obliged to live every day as if it's our last. But many people feel so trapped they've forgotten how to be amazed by life.

Our guests come to the Tuscan retreat to have a glorious adventure. But many, under the influence of the time they spend together, have felt comfortable enough and bold enough to admit that their life feels like it has come to a screeching halt. Where did all the excitement go? They spent decades with one main purpose in their lives—raising their children. This role has defined them. Now that those children have moved on, they're left alone to face oversized question marks. *Who am I when I don't have to be a mother every moment of every day? What do I do now?* Often these questions spark fear and despair. Not to mention guilt, a mother's default setting. Trying to shake off that reaction was the subject of my last book, *Not Guilty*, a memoir on the (often really funny) chaos of being a working mother.

When I was on a publicity tour for that book several years ago, I had begun a speech on a small platform in a bookstore in front of about two hundred people. In the front row, I noticed a mother with twins who were fast asleep in a double stroller next to her.

No more than five minutes into a talk about maternal guilt that I thought was quite light and humorous, I heard crying. I glanced at the twins, but it was neither one of them—it was their mom. I tried to carry on, but her wails only became louder and finally I had to stop and ask her what was wrong. She managed to pull herself together enough to say that she, the mother of ten-month-old twins, had a terrible secret.

Oh no, I thought, *what is coming next?*

"Sometimes," and here she started to cry even harder, "sometimes I like one better than the other!"

Before I could react, a smartly dressed elderly lady stood up at the back of the crowd and announced with a wide grin that she had seven children and most of the time she didn't like any of them. The audience roared with laughter, including the young mom, who must have felt her guilt dissipate in an instant. I carried on with my talk, but I thought about this mother afterwards— and I've thought of her often in the years since.

Sometimes all it takes to get over that next hurdle is to understand that it's normal to have these feelings, that everyone has such moments. We are not alone. This is something all the women who come to my retreats realize as they sit around a fire, wrapped in wool blankets under a starlit Tuscan sky, while the strangers around them spill out their hearts. Soon they find themselves sharing their own hearts too.

Instead of a Tuscan night around a fire, I hope in this book to offer you something almost as good! Also, over the years I have devised a list of questions for my guests to help them find the answers they seek. They don't do this in public, and there's no obligation on them to share their answers. But many of them have told me that facing these questions later, alone in their room, is a crucial first step to waking themselves up and remembering that life only runs one way.

So here are my questions. Grab a coffee or a glass of wine and find a quiet place away from other people . . . and away from your phone. I know it's hard, but try to be in the moment. Remember what happened to me in that Thai sauna and be prepared for anything. Intense, personal scrutiny can inspire a sense of reverence and possibility, but it can also spark fear and sadness. Being honest with yourself almost always produces startling results.

LIFE ONLY RUNS ONE WAY

Starter Questions

Be truthful in this next section.
Nobody is looking but you.

?

?

WHERE ARE YOU NOW?

Are you single and just starting out?

Are you in the middle of raising your family?

Are you about to become an empty nester?

Are you already an empty nester?

Are you divorced and on your own?

Are you headed towards a place you really want to be?

Is your life fulfilling?

Are you climbing the career ladder?

Do you ever ask yourself, "What's next for me?"

Are you in a happy place at work?

?

Are you in a relationship that's going nowhere?

?

?

?

What Is Your Present State of Mind? How did you feel last week, last month or over the last year? Circle as many as you need to describe your current state of mind.

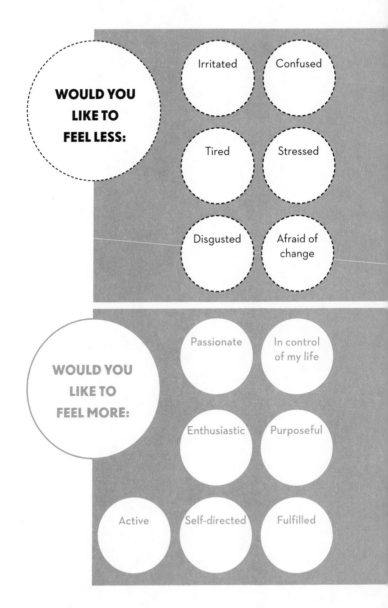

WOULD YOU LIKE TO FEEL LESS:

Irritated

Confused

Tired

Stressed

Disgusted

Afraid of change

WOULD YOU LIKE TO FEEL MORE:

Passionate

In control of my life

Enthusiastic

Purposeful

Active

Self-directed

Fulfilled

(Go back to these pages several months from now and see how you've changed.)

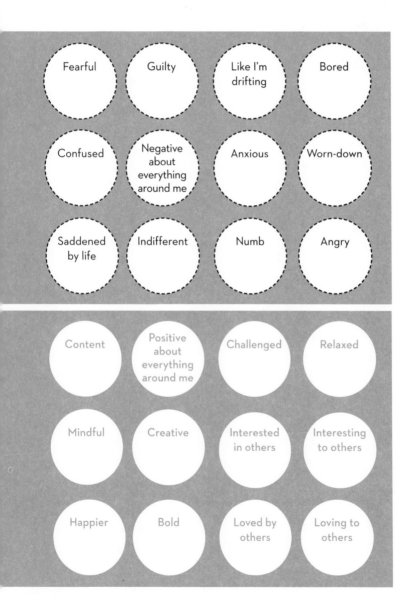

Fearful

Guilty

Like I'm drifting

Bored

Confused

Negative about everything around me

Anxious

Worn-down

Saddened by life

Indifferent

Numb

Angry

Content

Positive about everything around me

Challenged

Relaxed

Mindful

Creative

Interested in others

Interesting to others

Happier

Bold

Loved by others

Loving to others

DO YOU WANT TO SHAKE UP THE STATUS QUO?

Do you have a bucket list? ....

....

What crazy experience would you like to have?

....

....

Do unfamiliar experiences terrify you?...

....

....

Are you at a loss for an idea of where to go next?...

....

....

What job would you like to try?...

....

....

Would you like to start your own small business?...

....

....

Be your own boss? ....

....

Work with a friend to start something fresh? ....

....

Would you like to write, hike, sing, sew, paint, plant, talk, act, cook, build,

design? ....

....

Have you ever thought of taking up a new sport?.........................

....

Have you ever thought of moving to another country?.................

....

....

Have you dreamed of owning your own B & B? ....

....

What about running your own retreats?.......................................

....

....

DARE TO DREAM

Why should anyone listen to me on the subject of designing a brand-new chapter?

I have no credentials. I do really mean none—unless you count the diploma I received in Thailand after successfully completing a one-hour cooking class that guarantees I can make a superb curry.

I'm not a psychologist, nor have I ever burst through the glass ceiling as a corporate CEO. I'm not a life coach or even an advocate of self-help books—although I probably should have read a few more than I have.

I quit my all-girls school in the North of England at sixteen, and my teachers thought so little of my prospects they barely raised an eyebrow. Clearly they felt the way I did about any benefits I'd gain from more education.

It was mandatory at that school to have at least one session with the careers teacher—in my case a Miss Ramsbottom, whose name really was a pertinent description. After scanning my record, she told me there were three paths I might take.

"You could be a nurse," she said, looking dubious. Doing well in biology class was not my thing.

When I made no reply, she said, "What about a secretary?" I couldn't really see the appeal of that. Not to mention that my spelling was atrocious.

Finally, smirking as though this, too, was wildly improbable, she said, "Or you could get married."

Figuring I needed life skills, my desperate mother enrolled me in a local typing course. But when that didn't take, she actually rather calmly waved goodbye as I headed for the bright lights of London.

Ever since I left home at sixteen, I pursued each new job or opportunity with endless zeal. But I only felt that excitement if I loved what I was doing. As a young mother newly transported to Montreal from London, I had no friends, couldn't find a job and knew no one but my relatively fresh-from-the-altar husband. I spent my days nursing babies and painting our newly bought but old Victorian home. I discovered I loved houses—or at least I loved transforming them into something fabulous. Whether ancient, like the medieval tower and farm I've restored in Tuscany, or as bland as an eighties suburban ranch house, I see possibility everywhere. The high ceilings and endless white walls of our first marital home offered me a canvas where I could go wild, and I did.

When I'd married my Canadian, the paint effects trend was at its giddy height in the UK, but until I raised my paint-splattered head, it had not reached North America. You may have been lucky enough to have missed this vogue for transforming walls, floors, even furniture, with a plethora of sponges, rags, feathers, dragging brushes and floggers—oh, the imagination still soars. If you're in your twenties or thirties, you may have witnessed your mother high up a ladder when you got home from school, with *The Painted House* on the television in the background as she squished a sea sponge soaked in paint all over the living room walls. I admit I singlehandedly started the craze on this side of the Atlantic with my television series and decorating books. There was actually a scene in *Friends* where the cast are all watching *The Painted House*. The first time I was a guest on *The Oprah Winfrey Show*, she introduced me as "the queen of paint and plaster." And I really was just that . . . and I am sorry.

I apologize to all those who have had to sand down the bumps—vigorously—before they rolled over whatever notorious paint effect had been applied to their walls. I apologize to all the spouses who tried to turn a blind eye as their other half faux-marbled the washing machine (I am not joking—I have seen the pictures). I deeply apologize to the children who had their bedrooms transformed while they were away at camp for two weeks. I can still hear my youngest child yelling after he returned home from being a camp leader for the summer, "Mom, I really do not want a cowboy-themed bedroom. I'm fifteen!"

But, on another level, I am not at all sorry. I thrived on every minute of my decorating pilgrimage. Happiness comes from doing what sparks that knot of excitement and anticipation deep in your stomach. And I still remember how happy I was when we launched *The Painted House*—the first of a new entertainment genre that became known as lifestyle television—even though it premiered to a pathetic one hundred viewers on October 3, 1995. It turned out there was something else going on that was far more sensational than me in overalls slapping paint on a wall: on the very same day we first aired in the US and Canada, O.J. Simpson was found not guilty, after one of the most dramatic trials in US history. Even I did not watch the premiere of my own show because, like everyone else, I was glued to the news.

The following week, our numbers leapt and then kept growing. Records were set and bars were raised. The success of this series over the next seven years catapulted me and my team into the next show, *Facelift*. By then we were competing with an avalanche of similar series. When you are leading the pack, the wolves are constantly nibbling at your ankles and the pressure to stay at the top is relentless—from both the networks and the viewers. That pressure drove me for years. And, though after a long career and five different series, I've lost my excitement over being on television every day and meeting the challenges of that level of success, I still love to share my experience in a way that inspires others.

Now, when I greet the women who come to me in Tuscany, I feel exactly the same sensation I had when I demonstrated how to stencil an old chest of drawers on some talk show and watched the studio audience lean forward to absorb every word. I may not be a certified professional adviser but I have walked the walk, I have lived the dream and, in my time, I have dealt with many challenges and many moments when I realized I had to recalibrate my life.

Because of my own experience, I know that to tell you simply "Do what you love" is not enough. For one thing, in the early years of working for a living, that's rarely possible. Even if you've been lucky enough to follow a path you chose for yourself out of deep interest, there are always times when the passion for the job wears off and it becomes just a job. We might get to dream when we're young, but then reality sets in and reality can grind the dreamer right out of you.

I saw that as a teenager. North Lancashire was one of the most impoverished areas of the United Kingdom. At one time, its mill towns were the engine of the British industrial revolution, and the bedrock of Britain's prosperity, but after the Second World War many manufacturing companies began the move to far-off countries

PENGUIN POST

HANNELORE CUYPERS

One minute you are checking out your patient's teeth, the next you're running the world's most southerly post office.

Hannelore Cuypers' life took its first abrupt turn in 2009 when, after graduating from the University of Bergen in dentistry and opening a practice, she realized that she was unhappy with her chosen career. The money was good, but she found it tough to get out of bed and head to work each morning. "To keep me motivated, I began hiking in my spare time and felt an awakening from being outdoors and surrounded by nature," she said. Eventually she took a sabbatical from dentistry and embarked with a friend on a five-month, nearly three-thousand-kilometre trek in a remote area of Norway. "It was brutal," Hannelore told me. "We had horrendous weather, deep snow and no sun, plus we were camping along the way. But it changed me personally. After that, I knew I had to spend my time doing something that was important to me."

At thirty-two, Hannelore became the base leader for the UK Antarctic Heritage Trust museum and heritage site in Port Lockroy on Goudier Island, which lies just off the Northern Antarctic Peninsula. From November to March, Hannelore lived with a team whose duties are to look after the museum and the surrounding site, which includes picking up penguin poo, and to run the little post office, which stamps and sends out about eighty thousand postcards to more than a hundred countries every year. Her only other communication with the outside world was by satellite email. There is no running water, which meant that she only showered when the cruise ships that carry eighteen thousand tourists a year to the site invited the locals on board to use their facilities. The temperatures at Port Lockroy were often minus twenty degrees centigrade, and because of its position at the base of the globe, the norm is twenty-four hours of sunshine. Though Hannelore's stint at the post office has recently come to the end, she's totally devoted to a life in nature, far away from the dentist's chair.

looking for cheaper labour. The numbers of people who were unemployed grew steadily. My mother volunteered at the Citizens Advice Bureau, mostly counselling women trying to survive on welfare benefits or low-wage jobs, with deadbeat husbands and too much debt. I used to do my schoolwork sometimes in the corner of her office, and I remember the poster she had on her wall that laid out the priorities these women ignored at their peril.

From each paycheque, the poster said, first pay the rent, then the electric and gas bills. Next buy food. And only after all those essentials were taken care of could you spend what little was left on "other stuff." Some women in those days had one more challenge: at the end of the week, they had to grab their husband's pay packet *before* he walked across the road from the factory to the pub—and there was always a pub near the factory.

We may not be living with those kinds of challenges but, for most of us, taking care of these basics still comes first. When it comes to work, we're in it for one or more of these reasons:

1. We need to make a living.
2. We are, with luck, embarking on a career that we have trained for.
3. We hope to make a difference in the world.
4. We hope and need to be fulfilled.

Whether you are pouring coffee for a living or climbing the corporate ladder, you first need to put food on the table and pay for the roof over your head. If you have a job you believe is your future, or at least a stepping stone towards it, that's a bonus. If the work itself thrills and excites you every day, you've hit the jackpot.

We should all get medals for surviving what I think of as the "giddy years" when we're working, raising a family and trying to keep a relationship together all at the same time. But what happens when the giddiness passes, and every moment of your life isn't crammed to bursting with stuff you just have to get done? That's when you can dare to dream again.

Though those basic economic rules still stand, women today expect more from their lives, too. The women in my life, at least, are a different breed than their mothers and grandmothers were: They are healthier for longer, more active, more travelled. When their working lives are over, they want more than a quiet retirement, knitting booties for the grandchildren while hubby circles the house on his lawnmower. They think they deserve more than that, too.

By the time my mother was thirty-four, she was widowed and raising four kids on her own. Laundry on a Monday, baking on a Tuesday, cooking and freezing the same old meals for the week on a . . .

Well, you get the picture. Feminism had definitely not reached the North of England and, if it had, I doubt she would have had time for all that "faffing around," as she would have called it. To say my mother was happy cleaning the loos, feeding the lodgers she had to take in after my dad died, and endlessly ironing would be untrue, but her life was the norm where I grew up.

Undeniably, women still have a long way to go—and so many women in the world live lives much harder and more constrained than my mother's was—but many of us are faced with an abundance of opportunities not available to previous generations of women. Many of us have decent choices.

And then there's what we have experienced in our lives, so exotic and luxurious in comparison to what women of my mother's generation experienced. I remember taking my mom to a sushi restaurant when she was in her late forties; she was still telling her friends years later about the horror of being served little pieces of raw fish. "Actually not cooked," she would exclaim to her neighbour over the garden fence, and laugh. Heavens knows what she would think today about quinoa, wheatgrass shots or raw vegetables dipped in olive oil! My mother would cook French beans until they resembled a type of green porridge. The fact that they were called "French" was about as fancy as she could take.

Today, we are the beneficiaries of a movement and a social shift that has made a career a given for many women. Still, a lot of us have spent decades climbing the ranks in pursuit of our goals, only to face a sudden feeling of emptiness. We've been around the block, and work challenges no longer energize us the way they used to. We feel a sense of déjà vu—we've been there and seen all that. New hires look like teenagers. How can your boss be twenty years younger than you?—and is he actually wearing braces?

Your children have fled the nest without a backward glance, and home is now far too quiet; you're ashamed of your tears and loneliness and lack of purpose. You may be irrelevant in their lives as they immerse themselves in university and jobs, but you soon discover the wonders of technology. I love Skype because you can lay eyes on your kids wherever they are in the world for free. (Though I did overhear my youngest telling his brother, "Just don't show Mom how to use it." I mastered Skype on my own, thank you very much.)

Recently I Skyped my son who works in disaster relief, and instead of picking up, he typed, "Is everything okay? Can't talk. I'm in a board meeting at the UN."

I typed back, "I was just wondering if you've worked on your Christmas present list yet. I think Uncle Will would like this new book about a man who cuts wood in the nude in Norway that I heard about on the radio. Sounds hilarious."

What he wrote back was rather too colourful to print here, but it was something along the lines of "Mom, it's only July. I'm super busy—are you bored?"

Technologically staying in touch is grand, but the kids *are* gone. We are no longer a "we"—they have their own bills to pay and their own holidays to organize.

Of course, this is the way it should be—the way it must be—but you still sob into your early morning coffee with no breakfast dishes to clean up, no shoes to trip over and beds that are for once neatly made.

MORE FOOD FOR THOUGHT

SHARON HAPTON

Guests visit our place in Tuscany to be inspired, but I am often the one who is blown away by their stories. Especially Sharon Hapton's. There we were, rolling out worms of pasta known as *pici* (delicious when served with a thick tomato sauce), when she told the group about an electrifying moment she'd had while out for her daily walk.

"It was just before my fiftieth birthday, and I was feeling very low," she said. "My three sons had all left for college, and it was as if half my body had walked out the door. I needed to fill a giant void in my life.

"As I strolled along, I was thinking of all the good times our family had enjoyed together. All my memories seemed to be in the kitchen. I remembered cooking together with our friends and our kids over the years and enjoying the meals we made, and I felt an overwhelming sense of warmth. I had what Oprah calls an 'aha moment.'

"I realized I had been making soup for years as a way to nourish my children and to help friends and neighbours in need. 'I am a soup maker,' I thought. I wasn't sure but I may have said it out loud!"

She told us that for her fiftieth birthday, she held a soup-making party in a commercial kitchen near where she lives in Calgary, and everyone who attended went home with a couple of litres of wonderful soup for their families. Sharon was hooked: this would be the basis of her next chapter. "You cannot underestimate all the things you've been and the skills you've mastered over different times in your life and how each of those experiences can come together and support you later on," she said. Her next chapter became the non-profit organization, Soup Sisters.

"When Soup Sisters materialized, my life took on such meaning," Sharon said. It began with women coming to cook together for an evening, paying a small fee that went towards the rental of the kitchen and good quality ingredients. They chopped, diced, stirred and then ladled hundreds of litres of soup into containers that were then distributed to women in crisis at local shelters.

"It is a hug in a bowl," Sharon told us. (All pasta rolling had now ceased in my kitchen as some of the group were crying into their dough.) "It provides the moral support and nurturing message that they are not alone," she went on. "These women have arrived at the shelter after fleeing someone who was supposed to love them and they need to replace a little of that love, even if it comes from the healing power of homemade soup."

Ten years on, Soup Sisters has made and delivered well over 1.5 million servings of soup to women in shelters and teens in crisis. There are now twenty-five groups across Canada and the United States and Sharon and her team have published three books to share the many soup recipes with us all. She told us that during the first year she kept it small, but by the second year she had perfected the formula that the charity could then roll out. And men, called Broth Brothers, have been stirred into the mix. "They are amazing," she said. "They take their soup making very seriously."

Mixing fun and philanthropy was Sharon Hapton's recipe for success.

It is a terrible feeling, that cavern of maternal loneliness. And if you're also in a situation where your job is
no longer interesting, and your energy has faded when
it comes to fighting to get to the top, and no one really
seems to see you if you're over thirty-nine, you can feel
desperate.

And there are other stresses aging women face. A
close friend of mine actually burst into tears one morning in our local café, confessing that she felt like her life
was over. As she'd walked down the street with her
fourteen-year-old daughter, she'd realized that the swiv-
elling glances of appreciation coming their way were
now for her leggy teen. My friend is still completely
beautiful, for what that's worth, but the reality of no
longer being "seen" in the way she had become used to
being seen totally undermined her.

Women who are approaching middle age, well into
it, or moving beyond it experience a series of shocks to
their expectations that can send them into a tailspin and
on a search for new meaning and purpose in their lives.

These ages and moments of transition can be torture,
but they are also a time to soar. We need to realize that
we are still vital and have the brains and know-how
to tackle anything: We can be empowered by our own
experiences. What we don't know, we can learn.

Think of the leap Lucy Kellaway has made. For more
than thirty years, Lucy was a columnist at the *Financial
Times*. "I had the best job in the world," she says. "I wrote

about the bullshit in the corporate world and since there is so much bullshit I never ran out of things to say." But in 2017, at the age of fifty-eight, Lucy began a completely new chapter as a math teacher at an inner-city school in the UK—moving from a senior position at a major newspaper to the bottom rung of the ladder in the state school system.

But that is not all. Lucy also co-founded an educational charity, Teach Now, to support others who decide to quit their often high-ranking careers to go back to school to teach. Lawyers, doctors and financiers have given up their high-status jobs to give back.

Brave? Nuts? I am dazzled by Lucy's reasoning. She told me that she realized she was no longer getting better at what she did: "We all love the learning curve but after twenty years in one role you've usually stopped learning anything new. Thirty years will leave you screaming." She wanted to do something useful while she still had the energy. She asked herself what she really wanted at this stage in her life—and the answer was, she wanted to teach math. "Teaching in an inner-city school can be brutal," she told me. "I used to command respect and now I am a lowly junior teacher. But there is a simplicity in being at the bottom and I am now responsible for my own everyday learning." She has had to dip into her savings because her teaching salary is a mere fraction of her previous wage, but she is now so busy she jokes she has little time for discretionary spending anyway. She told me that many of her contemporaries have asked her about how she sustains the high energy she needs for the job, but she tells them that the teachers who have it the hardest are actually the ones with young families at home. She has an abundance of energy because, at this stage in her life, her evenings are her own and she can do what she needs to take care of herself. "The most difficult part of the job is also the best," she says. "The teaching itself."

So if Lucy can do it, why not you? So what if there are more creases around your eyes? When Mae West complained to a friend that she hated her crow's feet, the friend told her that they were just laughter lines. "Nothing is that funny!" she replied. But seriously, who cares?

If we're lucky, we are at a point in life where we can afford to take a risk on doing something completely different. Time is now on your side, and you've got loads more to spare since the free taxi service you offered the family for the last decade and a half has closed for business. The weekends spent on windy playing fields watching your beloved child attempt to score—gone. Along with the 2 a.m. calls to pick them up outside some club that sent you out to the car in your pyjamas. And don't forget the meals. The *thousands* of meals that you shopped for, prepared and cleaned up after.

Seriously, how many loads of dirty plates have you stacked and unstacked in the dishwasher during the lifespan of your family?

NEVER TOO OLD

TRICIA CUSDEN

L ast year I was hurtling through the Italian country-side with the radio tuned to a British station, listening to an interview with a woman who had started a hugely successful business out of nowhere. She was so riveting I stopped the car, wrote down her details and the next time I went to London, I called her and asked if we could meet. I am so glad I did.

Tricia Cusden is seventy, elegant, smart and with a sense of mission and an amount of energy that is empowering. She opened our conversation with this statement: "There has never been a better time to be an older woman. We are fitter, healthier and living longer than any time in history."

Only five years earlier, she might not have felt that way. Life was desperately challenging for Tricia, who was divorced, retired and bored. Then a tragedy landed on top of her. Her granddaughter became traumatically ill—unlikely to survive, according to the specialists—and Tricia spent the following year helping her daughter nurse her child.

It was touch and go for a very long time, but the little girl made a remarkable recovery. The family emerged from the fog and normal daily life once again took over. But as Tricia told me with a laugh, "I was not ready to go back to the sofa and that bloody television." The scary and awful passage with her granddaughter turned into the catalyst that catapulted her into a whole new life.

Before she retired, she had worked as a consultant for a management company. She didn't want to go back to that, and had no clue where she wanted to direct her renewed drive until she took a trip through the cosmetics section of a department store. The anti-aging messaging and products everywhere soon had her raging. She found she was deeply offended. "I was happy with my mid-sixties face," she said, "and I had no desire to turn back the clock with some miracle cream. What I craved was cosmetics designed for my age group." But no one was really doing that, so she thought, *Why not me?*

Soon Tricia found a manufacturer to help her create makeup for more mature skin. She took a close look at her savings and decided to use some of it to make several how-to videos using herself as the model to demonstrate makeup application for older faces. Then she launched them on YouTube and hit the niche dead-on: her videos immediately attracted thousands of women from all over the world. Her brand, Look Fabulous Forever, was now on the map.

Soon she had an online shop up and selling her makeup line globally. But, as she says, she was eager for Look Fabulous Forever to be about more than just makeup. She wanted to create a revolution in the way older women feel about their faces and their age. She now writes weekly blogs and has built a platform where like-minded women can chat together. She beamed at me as she said, "Who cares about the odd age spot or wrinkle. We just want to look fabulous, forever." We sure do. Right after our interview, Tricia got on a plane to Los Angeles where her products were being added to the gift bags for the stars at the Oscars. Now that is one empowered "granny."

If you think she must have had a huge team behind her and masses of capital, you're wrong. She began her multi-million dollar business with an investment of $70,000 from her savings, money she calculated she could afford to lose without risking becoming destitute. She worked out of her home and was the one who learned all the technology and social media she needed to grow her company.

Her two daughters have now joined her in the business. They are a small team and they are growing. How inspiring is that?

Now you have the luxury of eating an apple and a piece of cheese for dinner because that is what you feel like. That game box thingy is stored away in a basement cupboard and you have reclaimed the television remote control. And, most important, against all popular belief about how age diminishes us, as Lucy pointed out, you just might have more energy than you did when you were in the thick of raising a family.

The house may sound eerily quiet at those formerly deafening times of day (which often involved you standing at the bottom of the stairs screaming for your beloved children to get a move on or they would be late). So cry about it, sure. Change is hard and letting go of all those things you learned how to be for your children is especially hard. But then take a deep breath, and let another thought creep in: It is now *your* time, and yours alone. You have a chance to pick up where your younger self left off—or find a whole new road to journey down.

There is something else to consider: we are all living much longer.

There are life-expectancy calculators online now on which we can work out how long we are expected to be on this earth. I filled out the very basic information required on one of the websites and was given a 75 percent chance to live to eighty-five. Not bad, although I did cheat on the amount of alcohol I consume. Oh, and I knocked a few pounds off my weight. Joking aside, if you take early retirement at fifty or fifty-five, you likely have another thirty or so years on the planet. How are you going to live those years? What kind of a life do you want to lead?

And don't let that excuse that you're too old to try something new get in your way. As I write this, a new scientific study from neurobiological researchers at Columbia University has just come out that shows that older men and women who are in good health can produce just as many new brain cells as young people. So I guess I can't blame my pathetic inability to learn Italian on my aging brain! Seriously, if you are healthy and active, physically and mentally, there's no reason why you shouldn't try something new no matter your age.

It's time to dream it, do it and live it.

WHAT KIND OF A LIFE DO YOU WANT TO LEAD?

DREAM IT.
DO IT.
LIVE IT.

Imagine what it must it be like to tumble out of a plane. For an adrenaline junkie, skydiving might be the ultimate thrill, even if the rest of us think the whole idea is terrifying.

Some of us might *dream it*, but only as a momentary fantasy we never intend to pursue. But for others the dream grows wings—they can't stop thinking about what it would be like to soar like a bird.

So they move on from dreaming and actually *do it*: they find the school, book the appointment, start the training.

I've never jumped out of a plane, but I know you need to plan, practise, learn and listen. Only then do you leap.

And then you *live it*. Once out of that plane door, there's no going back, for better or for worse. The jump could be life-changing in the best possible way. Exhilarating. It could give you immense confidence and flood your mind with a stream of new and challenging ideas. After all, if you can jump out of a plane you can do anything.

But if things don't go as planned, your future may be very different. (You may end up a squashed tomato on the sidewalk!)

Whatever leap into the unknown you decide to take, you will live with the very real consequences.

DREAM IT

FOLLOW YOUR DREAMS.
THEY KNOW THE WAY

Dreams cost nothing, they have no calories, and they are wonderfully private. All of us dream. Babies dream, animals dream. Is there anything sweeter than watching a dog, flaked out by the fire, running free in its dreams, or a baby smiling in her sleep? We can dream anywhere, and not just at night. We can daydream or indulge in wishful thinking, playing with a million ideas that most of us will never act on.

"What would it be like if one day I had my own little store, or went to work in an exotic country, or opened a rustic beach bar on a sun-drenched island?"

Your mind chatters as you lie at the end of a yoga class in a savasana pose: "What if I took yoga more seriously and opened up my own studio one day?"

"Imagine if I could sell home-cooked meals to overworked mothers," you wonder as your family eats your famous homemade stew and tells you, "You should market this, Mom—it's amazing." Maybe you should, you think to yourself.

Your mind wanders in the boardroom as you silently debate starting your own accounting firm. After all, you can do this job in your sleep. What if these people were your personal clients and you could work your own hours? Even from home?

Stuck in an endless meeting, you fantasize about being your own boss. That lovely bed and breakfast you walk past each day seems to be doing a roaring business. You can make a decent bed and are known for your delicious breakfasts. What if you turned the family cottage into your own B & B?

Then that ugly, unsupportive inner voice rises up.

"You could never afford to open your own business. What about your steady paycheque and taking care of the family?"

Then there are the worse thoughts:

"I don't have what it takes to pull this off."

"I'm not clever enough, pretty enough or thin enough."

"Where would I find clients and, even if I did, why would they want to hire me?"

"I don't have the confidence, the contacts or the guts to do my own thing."

"I will fail."

That voice of disapproval and doubt has a point. The kids do still need you, your bank account is pathetic and the mortgage is a stone around your neck. Maybe you will fail, and your peers might enjoy witnessing that. People who are stuck in their own ruts do like to judge. After all, "Who does she think she is?"

But all these doubts are mostly excuses to stay put. And I'm here to tell you that the most successful entrepreneurs have had countless conversations like these in their heads. I certainly have.

Even as I write, I am full of self-doubt and apprehension. Who am I to be creating this book when I only have a high-school education? Why didn't I listen in my English class instead of sketching pictures of my ideal boyfriend? I imagine my editor, Anne, reading my manuscript over her morning tea, horrified by my sometimes shaky grasp of grammar and spelling. Is she reading bits out loud and chuckling at the absurdity of me even trying to do this? ["Of course I'm not," Anne wrote in the margin of the manuscript. "Writers constantly doubt themselves."]

It's not only writers who constantly doubt themselves.

But that is why dreaming is so life-enhancing. Your dreams belong purely to you. They are yours to play with or to discard at will. No one will judge you for them.

And some dreams stick. They refuse to leave the party when the voice of reason tells you that you are useless, unqualified—only a romantic amateur. Instead of remaining a fantasy tucked inside your head, that dream insists on taking a firmer shape. Then comes the moment when you pluck up the courage and share that idea with someone else. When you say, *out loud,* "What if. . . ?

WHAT IF I FOLLOWED MY DREAM?

After the incident of the old man and the farmhouse lunch, I became fascinated by everything Italian. I read many books, but there was one in particular that obsessed me. I hid from my children in the bathroom to inhale every nurturing word. When the house was quiet after they'd finally gone to bed, I stayed up into the wee hours to read more, curled up on a sofa strewn with their homework, school books and chewed-up pencils. The tattered paperback of *Under the Tuscan Sun* felt like my own delicious secret.

I lived every moment with the author, Frances Mayes (who has now become a good friend; talk about a dream come true), as she undertook the fascinating adventure of buying a dilapidated villa in the hills of Tuscany and bringing it back to life. I read and reread page after dog-eared page, fantasizing about one day following in her footsteps. What if I unearthed a medieval stone sink from under an olive tree and had to explain to my very own cheery Italian architect that I wanted to install it in my Tuscan farmhouse kitchen, just as Frances had?

She wrote about the simple delights of eating bruschetta—basically toast and chopped tomatoes—but with homegrown, sun-kissed fruit from her Tuscan garden. I ran to my kitchen and sliced a supermarket one on top of some toasted bread. But where Frances' snack tasted of "a rich land and sunshine," mine was a bland, soggy nothing!

I underlined phrases and marked special passages. I laughed out loud at her encounters with her new neighbours. I wept alongside her when she was lonely and worried that her renovation had become so complicated and hard she would never finish. I understood the tribulations of living in a foreign language—I was an Englishwoman living in francophone Montreal—but I imagined I, too, could be like her and struggle through the language problems with gestures. I too could draw building plans in the dirt with a long stick surrounded by charming Tuscan builders. Through her prose, I "lived" under the Tuscan sun, like so many of her other readers. I can't count how many times I have sobbed through a Sunday afternoon glued to the movie made from the book. I wanted what Frances had, a house in Italy. It could be tiny, I didn't care. Just a stone shack on a Tuscan hillside would do as long as it had a line of cypress trees and neighbours called Luigi and Luca, who would leave eggs from their farmyard chickens on my doorstep and invite me over for heavenly meals under the setting sun.

I kept this dream in my heart, never sharing it with a soul. For years, I also felt foolish that reading Frances' book made me think I knew anything about life in Italy.

Then we travelled there to film some episodes for one of my television shows. Like so many before me, I was overwhelmed by the romance of the historic buildings, the hilltop villages built from butter-coloured stone, and the enchanting countryside. I understood why poets and writers have always been drawn here; the country's beauty constantly unfolds and feeds the soul. The light and the heady mix of smells, sounds and flavours capture even the most cynical imagination. Photos and movies never do this country justice, which I discovered the first time I saw it for myself.

Of course, Hans was there, too—he was directing the show! Early one evening we had some time alone after the crew had wandered off to explore. It was only the onset of spring, yet the weather was sunny and mild. We were in T-shirts as we sipped Campari and soda in a piazza in the medieval fortress town of Volterra. The waiter looked bemused as he regarded our bare arms— typically, the Italians were still in puffy jackets at this time of the year, whatever the weather. His face lit up when we told him we were filming in his beautiful country. Forgiving us for being underdressed foreigners, he left us to our drinks.

We sat in silence witnessing the world around us. Old men chatted passionately in animated groups, gesturing constantly, and teenagers sauntered around us as if re-enacting a part in a black-and-white Italian movie from the sixties, cigarettes dangling from the boys' lips as they flirted with the girls. We watched the barman mixing drinks while holding a loud and animated conversation with a friend across the square. I asked Hans what he thought they were talking about. "From the look of their smiles and gestures, I would say, a woman," he said, and laughed.

Then he became serious. He stared across the square and over the valley, a view miraculously unbroken by buildings apart from the odd farmhouse and the narrow, winding white roads that criss-cross Tuscany. "I love this place," he said, stroking my hand. "What if . . . ?"

It took those two short words to change my world forever. My secret daydream of buying a home in Tuscany gushed out, and my relief and excitement that Hans felt the same way had me breathless. By the end of the evening we were hugging and kissing and promising each other that we would just do it: find a place in Tuscany to call our own. "It takes two to tango" are the truest of words.

Then it was dawn, and our fantasy did not exactly die—it just cooled, given the crush of daily life and all its demands.

Still, over the next few years, we kept a notebook in which we listed places we should visit and people who'd already made the move to Italy—friends of friends of friends, and strangers too. We had begun the long, arduous search for our place.

The actor Michael Tucker, who starred in the TV hit series *L.A. Law*, had bought a place in Umbria and written a book about his experience, called *Living in a*

Foreign Language. I read it first, then handed it over to Hans on the plane as we headed to New York on business. By the time we landed, he'd decided he was going to call Tucker. "You can't just call up a TV star," I protested. How he found the number I will never know, but by that evening he had not only called Michael Tucker but he'd arranged to have drinks with him and his wife, the actress Jill Eikenberry, in the Mandarin Oriental Hotel. The four of us hit it off straight away and, a few months later, we visited these kind-hearted souls at their renovated farmhouse in Italy. We picnic-lunched amidst their olive trees and wild flowers, sipping over-filled glasses of Aperol spritzers. I felt I was in a scene from *A Room with a View*. By the time we waved goodbye to them, we were even more determined to follow in their footsteps. We spent weeks exploring and soon discovered that there was so much more to life in Italy than just a pretty house in the *campagna*. As Robert Browning wrote, "The people are more magical than the land."

We joined hordes of old men chatting outside the local village bars at *aperitivo* time. We visited bustling, local markets and watched townspeople share gossip, laughter and sometimes tears. Strangers invited us home for meals; it's heartening how sharing delicious food brings people together. We returned to Italy whenever we could, on the hunt for the perfect property. The search was as exhilarating as it was daunting. On these trips, we felt like newlyweds again.

We might have gone on happily searching forever, since there was no hurry, no deadline to bring this dream to fruition. But then I blurted out an impulsive declaration—in public—that would force us to realize our castle in the air.

In 2009, I was invited to be the keynote speaker at a women's event in Vancouver where I was interviewed on a stage by a local newscaster. We perched on two stools in a large theatre looking out over an audience of about nine hundred women—and a few men who probably wandered into the auditorium thinking I would be handing out some painting tips.

We chatted about my television shows and how I designed my product line, but decorating wasn't really on my mind. Instead, I wanted to discuss the challenges of juggling family and work. I was interested in sharing my thoughts on how accumulating money and power should not be the definition of a successful life and how important balance was to our overall happiness. Under astute questioning from my interviewer, I shared tips on how to put the demands of success in perspective. Then she threw me a curveball. I don't know why the question came as a surprise, but when she asked, "What is next for Debbie Travis?" I fell completely silent. Several long moments went by.

I have no clue where my answer came from, but I heard myself announcing that apart from a new prime-time series that I was about to start filming, I had another mission. I would be taking women from all walks of life and of all ages to a romantic villa in Tuscany where we would exchange stories, ideas and dreams for our next chapter. We would embrace the camaraderie of women and enjoy everything that is Tuscan: the people, the food and copious amounts of local wine. We would walk through the vineyards and picnic in the olive groves. Most of all, we would talk. I told the audience how much I adored this region of Italy and how joyous, calm, healthy and happy I felt when I was there. How it made me feel that my life was in balance.

The penny had dropped as I sat on that stage. I did not want to live the Tuscan expat dream or just visit for holidays. I wanted to start a new venture where I could share the *dolce vita* with others.

I looked out at all these people who had come to listen to me. No one moved. No one spoke. No one tweeted or texted. They just stared back at me. Then I heard a communal intake of breath—that kind of inhalation that comes from deep in the soul. Hands shot up in the air, and voices called, "Take me, take me." (Husbands wrote to me later saying, "Take her, take her!")

And I wanted to take them! The problem? I did not have a hut in Tuscany, let alone a villa.

So I went to see my best friend, Jacky, in London, and bravely asked her if she would quit her job and join me on this adventure. I have known her since our late teens (we met when we were both modelling in Tokyo) and she is my rock. I figured we would do this together or not at all. She smiled at me over her tuna salad and said, "Yes." She knew it meant giving up her job as part-owner in a building company. But she was finding it both challenging and mundane, and thought it was the right time for her to quit and turn the page.

Then we roped in our two beloved husbands to be the drivers and errand runners. Not an easy task, as Hans is a businessman who runs our television production company, and Steve is an award-winning record producer. But they both jumped in feet first. Within six months, we had rented a large property south of Siena where we hosted our first group of women. The dream I'd blurted out on the stage in Vancouver had turned into Debbie Travis' Tuscan Getaways. I loved everything about it.

After the success of the first getaway, although I was still fully involved in filming a TV series, we proceeded to hold one every year in the rented property as we carried on the search for a place of our own. Thankfully, we soon found and bought a beautifully situated but completely rundown farm and villa on a hundred acres of Tuscan farmland, which I renovated over the next five years. This is now our home—and the place where for part of the year we hold weekly retreats.

I had a dream and it came to fruition. I stepped into the world of *Under the Tuscan Sun* and made it my own. Along with holding the retreats, we harvest a thousand olive trees, nurse the struggling vineyard, hang out with our neighbours (a Luca and a Luigi among them) in the village bar and live this magical Tuscan lifestyle.

By now we have hosted hundreds of guests. Everyone comes with her own story. Many visit simply because Tuscany is on their bucket list. Once they arrive and embrace the magnetism of the place, and the company and support of the other women, they open up and talk. The conversational threads weaving through each group are pretty similar:

"What is next for me?"

"I have given so much to everyone else in my life, I don't remember who I am."

"Do I really have to spend twenty more years commuting to an office?"

"My job doesn't make me happy anymore and this has to change."

"I need to bring vitality and a sense of engagement back into my world."

"It's time for me to follow my dreams—if only I knew what they are."

"I have been through a serious illness, but I survived and now I have the energy to take on the world again. But what do I do?"

"For me life is no longer about money and status, it is about prioritizing what really matters to me."

Safely in the company of others in the Tuscan landscape, they are able to release emotions they clearly have been denying. By the end of the week, many of them are at last able to say what they wish for *themselves*, not for others. Many have a dream that has been growing, untended, for years. Others have rarely allowed themselves to dream because they've been so locked into the demands of careers, of marriage, of parenting.

And many of them resemble me in that Thai sauna: startled into realizing that they had forgotten what makes them happy, what they truly love, what they always wanted.

WHAT
IS
NEXT
FOR ME?

SEVEN WAYS TO FIND YOUR PASSION

C rucial to making a dream come true is finding your passion.

We discuss that word "passion" a great deal at our Tuscan getaways. Passion means different things to each of us. Mention the subject and some people will smile to themselves while others will look disheartened.

"Where did my passion go?" wailed one guest after her third glass of white wine. "It's fine for you to talk about finding your 'next chapter.' I know I'm bored and it is clear that I need to do something with my life, but I feel empty. Excitement for me is an evening with Netflix and a bag of chips."

Sounds good to me, I thought, but not if that is all there is.

Passion comes and goes and has peaks and lows. What we are passionate about as a young person is often not what lights up our life when we are older.

In my teens, I was bored with school and eager to leave home so I could do my own thing. I daydreamed relentlessly about the big-city lights and living solo in London—well away from the chaos of my large family. By the time I was seventeen, I was sharing a flat with some other young women in the city, out every night eagerly seeking the pulse of London. But now, many years later, at the end of a day, I often sit on a bench overlooking my sleepy Tuscan valley, experiencing the same awe and intensity of emotion I once felt sitting up top on a double-decker bus, dizzy with the joy of life in the big city.

So don't fall into the pattern of thinking that all that emotion and excitement is for other people, that it's too late for you and you have to settle. It's just not true.

Here are seven lessons to help you reignite your passion.

LESSON 1 WAKE THE CHILD IN YOU

I have yet to meet a child who is not passionate. Give a kid an empty box or a pile of sticks and their imagination will run riot. No matter how ground down you feel as you slog through your daily routine, I'm sure that you remember losing yourself in the unadulterated happiness of working on something you loved at some point in your life. Especially when you were a kid.

So I want you to revisit your childhood. Take an afternoon off, chase family and friends away and spend the time alone. Get out your photo albums and anything else that will spark a flood of memories. As you explore your personal landscape, remember the moments that made you laugh out loud. That delighted you, that thrilled you. Remember the innocent sensation of just being silly. Imagine the smells, the sounds and the textures of those times. It's so easy to lose our sense of self when we never take the time to think about ourselves: we have to *practise* to get back into the habit.

Start to play again. Bake some cookies just for you, dig in the garden, turn up the music and dance, do your nails a crazy colour, take a brisk walk, take a long bubble bath, paint a picture, paint a room, take a photograph of something you find beautiful, dress up and take a selfie, build something. Take a train to an unfamiliar stop, get off and explore a new place. Try talking to a stranger at the next table in a restaurant. Awkward, yes, but occasionally really rewarding. I met about half of the new friends I've made in Italy this way. Strip away all your obligations and just have fun.

Then do it again. Book an hour or two each week to play, to explore, to remember what you like. Just do it. If you let yourself really be yourself, you'll find out what makes you sing.

When I was twelve years old, we moved to a new house where, for the first time, I was given my own bedroom. The previous family sleeping arrangements had been me on the top bunk with my two younger sisters squished in the bed below me—a nightmare. (We were three sisters close in age who bickered wildly, though we were friends again minutes later.)

But this new room was all mine. It was tiny—so small it had originally housed a toilet (in UK homes in the early seventies, the loo was often in its own separate room apart from the bathroom with tub). My mother told me I could do whatever I wanted in that ten-by-eight-foot cell. Even though she was heavily pregnant with my brother at the time, she worked alongside me as we ripped out the rotting linoleum and the stinking, soggy wood floor underneath. We laid fresh planks, then topped them with a patchwork of mismatched carpet ends we'd found in a discount store. It was not exactly what decorating shows are made of, but I was beside myself with glee. I painted the walls and the ceiling a shiny, pillar-box red and splattered them with posters. I changed it up every few months, and the only comment my parents made was their raised eyebrows. There's no question where my passion for painting and decorating came from.

A few years later, I remember we went for a family visit to some cousins who, as my mum would say, were "flush with money"—rich in our eyes but probably just comfortably well off. They did have a lovely big house that I briefly mistook for a hotel. And when we arrived at the end of the long driveway, the family was lined up to greet us. Not exactly *Downton Abbey*, but it was posh.

I remember how my aunt's face radiated happiness as she showed us to our guest rooms. In mine, she'd laid fresh towels on the bed and set a vase of wild flowers atop the hand-painted bureau. I'd never been in such a room. Our house was wonderful, but it was a practical home suited to a large family. In this enchanting guest room, I felt special—delighted that she'd fluffed it up just for me.

Four decades later, I escort every guest who comes to Tuscany to her room myself. They are often quite surprised that the person they recognize from television is the one showing them around their suite. I am sure I radiate as much pride as my aunt did, given that I designed each room with one mission—to make everyone who stays in it feel as special and as cared for as I felt all those years ago.

Adulthood tends to squash childhood passions. To rekindle your joy, explore your past—and pay special attention to what delighted you as a child. Something that thrilled you, years ago, could shape a new chapter today.

Childhood Dreams

Lynne came to the first retreat I held in our renovated villa in Tuscany. I knew she was a high-powered executive, but she was quiet and thoughtful during her first days with us. At the forum every evening, as the rest of us shared stories, confessing our frustrations, challenges and dreams over Prosecco in a setting that was both magical in feel and deeply nonjudgmental in tone, she was one of the few to hold back. We were two-thirds through the week when she finally broke her silence.

Lynne told us that she had always done everything that was expected of her to the best of her ability. She had excelled at school and university, and at work. "I have been at the same job, in the same building, with many of the same colleagues for nearly twenty years," she said. "I loved the challenges of my everyday work life and put my entire world into this role." She had never married or had children, and confided that she had few friends—the endless hours she spent on her job made socializing tough.

But now she was forty-nine years old, with the big five-o looming. Recently she had begun to wake each morning with a sense of dread. She did not look forward to the day ahead and had little joy in her life, at home or in the office. "I have a good job that I have worked hard at," she said. "I have a healthy salary and I own my own condo but I am bored and I am lonely." And then she cried. Of course, we all cried with her.

"What is it you would like to do?" one woman asked.

"What makes you happy? What makes you smile?" another wanted to know.

Lynne actually had an answer. She told us that when she was a little girl she would spend endless hours lying on her back gazing at the stars with her father, whose passion was astronomy. These were her happiest memories. She grew up and left home, and her father died, and in time the thrill of these childhood sessions became a distant memory. As she spoke, we all noticed that her face became as illuminated as one of those stars she'd studied so many years ago.

"So why don't you just do it?" someone exclaimed.

Not so easy, she said. What about her job security, her mortgage? Who would look after her mother, who was elderly and on her own?

These are the kind of questions that grind any thoughts of change to dust. But they were questions Lynne needed to answer.

Three months after she flew home from her week in Tuscany, I received an email from her. She told me she was in the Antarctic on a trawler with eighteen hunky men, studying the stars. Seriously, you could have knocked me over with a penguin feather. She explained that after the retreat she had met with an adviser who had created a financial plan so she could take a year's sabbatical from her job. Then she'd asked her company for the time off, and received the okay.

After that year away, Lynne was a new woman. She did not become an astronomer, but the experience in Antarctica reignited her passion for life. Eventually she left her old job altogether and began a consulting company, where she is her own boss and can take the time she needs to look out for her own happiness. She now travels the world, pursuing her fascination with the solar system as a hobby.

LESSON **HOW TO GROW THE SEED OF AN IDEA**

My father was an engineer who designed and produced machines to make candy for the big candy corporations, like my very own Willy Wonka. He manufactured vast cauldrons in which he and his colleagues would create a variety of sweets, including many famous brands. As a kid, I would sneak my friends into the factory to watch the workers make our favourite candy, the gobstopper or jawbreaker. We weren't supposed to be there, but occasionally a kindly man would ignore us young trespassers when we snuck in, even toss us a few delicious hard candies. Most of the time, though, we were told to bugger off.

I always came back, though. I found the process of making gobstoppers mesmerizing. A seed the size of a flea was dropped into a whirling vat, followed by liquid sugar in a neon colour only a child would adore. As the seed spun around and around, the sugar syrup coated it and dried. This process was repeated with a wild variety of crazy colours until the layers of sugar had enlarged the tiny seed to the size of a ping-pong ball. Out in the world, a kid somewhere would stick that gobstopper in her mouth and ruthlessly suck, dissolving the rock-hard layers until the seed was once again revealed. The challenge with a gobstopper was never to crunch.

What has making gobstoppers got to do with finding your next chapter?

Well, you start with a tiny idea that you mull over in your head. It is your private dream, small and delicate.

Then you add layers, and your confidence grows one coat at a time. Even that very first layer helps you find the courage to tell a friend, a sibling or a partner about your dream. You worry, because it's still fragile, and people could laugh at you. But no, they think it's a good idea, which adds another layer. You test out your idea on more people, and still more, until it no longer seems so fragile and private and silly. Soon you have gone from dream to *what if* . . .

Seeds of Happiness

Judy, a guest at a recent Tuscan getaway, kept disappearing. We always found her perched on an old wooden bench in the *orto*. (This delicious Italian word means vegetable garden.) My garden is a hit, not only because it provides a year-round supply of succulent veggies but because it looks like it just popped out of the pages of *House & Garden* magazine. I have surrounded it with a woven willow fence similar to the British ones I always admired. The raised beds are made from weathered planks. It is a dreamy place to just sit and think, and that is what Judy did, often. She told me that hanging out in the garden was the highlight of her week.

I assumed she liked it so much because she was nibbling on the sweet cherry tomatoes or the crunchy fennel but, no, my garden gave her motivation for a life-changing decision. Judy decided to sell her downtown home, move to the country and grow vegetables. When she got back, she moved fast. Within a few months, she was selling her produce on a stall at a farmers' market several hours from the city she used to live in and she was happy. She found her passion in my little patch of veggies.

I love this story because it is so uncomplicated. Often the simplest ideas bring the most happiness.

LESSON 3 HOW TO CAPTURE YOUR DREAM—WRITE IT DOWN!

You probably already have a steady stream of possibilities whirling in your brain—ideas and little inklings you squash quickly or forget. I highly recommend jotting down these thoughts as you have them. I send myself a constant stream of emails with "a new idea" in the subject line. I have hundreds.

Email might not work for you, so use whatever means suits you best. Scraps of paper you tuck in a folder, your phone's dictation function or a good old-fashioned notebook.

Step outside your usual working mode and be creative with these notes. Let your mind wander. Don't worry about the wording or refining the idea at this point. Be as candid as you can be. Think of this as an "ideas" vacation—anything goes.

And don't give up if nothing comes the first time you try this. Sometimes we can be shy with ourselves (no, I can't be thinking *that*). Sometimes we're just rusty at the whole act of expressing what we mean. Give yourself time. Try again if at first you don't succeed, and be open-minded.

Take your worries and doubts and put them down on paper, too. I find that writing down my fears helps eliminate the noise in my head. It also helps put stress and worry in perspective. More on this soon.

The Life List

The Tonsleys is a tiny neighbourhood in south London where I live part of the year. Nearby is a quaint row of Victorian shops and amongst them a brightly painted charity store selling second-hand designer clothing. I wandered in one day and was taken aback when a smartly dressed lady in her sixties asked me for an autograph—a rare occurrence in England as I am unknown there. It turned out that the clerk, Beverley, was a Canadian from Nova Scotia.

I can't help being curious, so I asked her what had brought her all the way from Canada to a job in a charity shop in London.

It turned out her daughter had married a Brit and settled in London. Beverley had been widowed and was lonely back home. After her daughter gave birth to twins, she visited regularly—as a grandma, she wanted to be useful. But she was still forlorn. One night over supper in their kitchen, she broke down and confessed that she felt bored, isolated and old, even in the midst of her daughter's busy, lively household.

Her son-in-law suggested pen and paper might help. Shoving the plates and cutlery aside, he asked her to be impulsive and write down what she liked, what made her feel alive and fulfilled.

She didn't have to think twice. Her top two items: "I enjoy meeting new people. I am passionate about clothes." Sitting around the table, the family discussed her options.

While a job at a trendy boutique was unlikely to materialize at her age, the charity shop had just opened around the corner.

The next day, Beverley marched in, offered her services and was hired on the spot. Now, four years later, she runs a team of women in eight different locations across the city and spends her days receiving donated clothes, hearing the stories of each piece from the owners and helping others enjoy their finds. In her mid-sixties, Beverley moved full time to the UK and bought herself a flat near her daughter's house; she has made numerous friends through her time in the shop. All thanks to putting pen to paper.

Writing stuff down gave her not only clarity but a new lease on life.

LESSON 4 TAKE A TIP FROM A DESIGNER

You've probably watched enough decorating shows to know that when a designer is putting a room together, her prime tool is a mood, creativity or vision board. Whatever it's called, it's simply a collage of pictures or articles that inspire you.

Put up a large poster board on a wall and pin up anything that speaks to you. Make sure you hang it in a place you pass every day, not down in a basement storage room or in a spare room you rarely use. You will be amazed at how simply glancing at these images as you pass by will feed your daily musings.

There has been much written about "the law of attraction" (some of it highly critical), but I do feel there is something positive in the idea. If you stare at a picture of a Ferrari for a year, it is unlikely to materialize in your driveway, but taking the time to daydream over images that are significant to you will spark your imagination and set you thinking about how you can make them a reality in your life. The very physicality of the board—actual pictures printed and hung in close proximity so you can see all the ways they overlap and feed each other—is important to the process. In my experience, swishing through your Pinterest or Instagram likes doesn't have quite the same effect.

When we were house-hunting in Italy, I had a strong sense of what I was searching for. My vision board, which I hung above my desk in the office, was covered with tearsheets of houses in the South of France, Italy, even Morocco. I stuck up a picture of a lavender field in Provence. There was a shot of a Moorish building with soaring romantic arches. I wanted arches. I had a sketch of an antique metal table set for lunch under an olive tree. That would do. I must have stared at these images, and more, a thousand times as I daydreamed about the future instead of concentrating on the present television production.

The search for an actual place wasn't quite so dreamy. The local real estate agents got royally fed up with criss-crossing the region to show me a variety of old convents, mills and rundown farms, only to have me reject them all. I was insisting that each item on my wish list had to be checked off.

After months of touring derelict buildings, Hans and I were heartily sick of viewing yet another crumbling farm with filthy mattresses on the stone floors and faded girlie posters from the 1960s adorning every wall, including those in the stable. We were discouraged by kitchens that had not seen a mop for decades, which came complete with a toothless granny silently rocking by the open fire and maybe hoping she would go with the sale. We checked out medieval castles that looked beautiful in photos but actually needed to be demolished and rebuilt. Even if we'd wanted to take one on, there were so many family members with claims on the ownership, it would take years to get them all to sign off on our offer. We'd seen old mills, too, with oodles of potential, except that they were always in the river valley bottoms and were often dark and damp. We toured convents on the market, stunning places with an abundance of arches. But they often had elderly nuns still living within their medieval walls and, if we bought the place, we would have to make endless trips to the Vatican petitioning for permission to relocate them. Even in pursuit of my dream, I was not up to evicting nuns.

Still, we kept searching, enlisting whichever agent had any patience left. When we arrived at the Tuscan property that eventually became our home, I refused to get out of the car. It was raining and all I could see was a rundown farmhouse that looked nothing like my vision board. But Hans had already visited the place twice without me and he insisted there was something here for us.

To humour him, I slogged through the muddy farmyard into the shelter of the crumbling stables, which in the Tuscan style were on the ground floor of the main building. The space was huge. Squinting through a haze of dust and cobwebs, I surveyed the mounds of broken farm equipment and the mouldy salamis and ham hocks hanging from the beams. A river of evil-smelling brown stuff ran along a trough in the middle of the dirt floor. The few windows that were not broken were so thick with grime that even the relentless rain could not reveal "a room with a view." The source of the stench, an enormous pig, lay in his corner watching us closely.

My shoes were ruined, my clothes soaked. I was cold and in the foulest of moods. Hans ignored my misery and pointed through the gloom. There, rising above us, were eight original brick arches. "Looks like the picture on your vision board," he beamed.

"Well, not quite," I growled, but the seed was already taking root.

We wandered outside. Magically, the rain ceased and there before us was the quintessential Tuscan valley drenched in golden light. The property was a tiny kingdom of outhouses, pigsties and barns that popped out of the mist, tilting precariously, walls partially missing and roofs collapsed. Renovated, they would become private suites for our guests, each with its own little garden. A vacant field of rough pasture sloped towards us. That would be ideal for planting lavender, I thought. A grove of olive trees stretched into the distance; any one of those sprawling trees would welcome that picnic table I had stared at for months.

We bought the property. I still have that vision board rolled up somewhere. If I took a look at it now, it probably would be like looking at my dream made real.

Surround yourself with images that inspire you. You might take an unlikely path to realizing your dream, but just as I did, when you get to the end of your journey you'll recognize the place in which you've arrived.

LESSON 5 — HOW TO FIND YOUR INSPIRATION

You know that you need to make a change, but all you see inside your head when you try to imagine what the change could be is a formless, anxiety-producing blank space. How do you make a vision board of that?

It's easy for me to say "Just follow your passion." But what do you do if you've come to a place in your life where you are not only clueless as to what that passion might be but defeated by the status quo?

"Yes, my life is dull, but there's not much I can do about it."

"I go on social media, and I get depressed because everyone seems to be having a more interesting time than me."

It is true, Facebook, Instagram and the rest of the social media platforms are a competitive maze of images of everyone seemingly having a more fascinating life than you. Who wouldn't find it painful—like salt rubbed into the wound of an ordinary life? How do we remain content in our daily routine when our friends seem to be constantly on a tropical beach somewhere, looking suspiciously over-filtered and Photoshopped slender in their bathing suits.

Pause the social media if it bothers you and spend the time, instead, seeking out and being inspired by real stories of real next chapters. Read, watch and listen to the journeys of others. Find out everything you can about their particular ventures—what inspired them and how they pulled it off—and I promise that their fervour will be contagious. I get inspired watching TED Talks, for instance—the ones where "ordinary" people explain in twenty powerful minutes how they have risen to a challenge and done something extraordinary, often for the good of others.

Then take the next step: contact someone who motivates you and aim to meet him or her in person.

This sounds terrifying, I know, but you'll be amazed at the response you get. I have screwed up my courage to do this all my life, from before the time where some people, at least, would recognize my name. Just pick up the phone and ask if you can have a moment of the person's time to ask a couple of questions. Or reach out to them by private message on Twitter or other social media. Or attend a seminar and approach the speaker afterwards. Offer a business card, and follow up with a couple of clear and precise questions. The very worst that can happen is you'll be told to take a hike, but I've found that this response is rare. People who have made their dreams come true, who have found their calling or launched new businesses, are usually open to sharing their personal stories because they are evangelical about the whole idea of forging your own path.

I said I would come back to Frances Mayes, whose book inspired me to find my own new chapter.

After we bought our pile of Italian stone, we began the arduous marathon of a five-year renovation. A tsunami of lists washed over us and were slapped to every surface. There were architects and builders to hire, numerous permits to apply for, equipment to rent—even a crane so huge it would fit into the cavity of the foundation of a city high-rise. Along with the hundreds of truckloads of concrete, the crane had to be manoeuvred onto the site down a steep gravel road.

Added to the daily theatrics of the building site, which accommodated up to eighty workers on any given day, I had to find a roof over my head, as ours had been removed. For months, as Hans was back at home handling the daily business of our production company, I lived alone in a small flat in a neighbouring village, with no one in my time zone I could call up and ask for help, while I dealt with a torrent of questions, from where to find tiles and stone for floors to who could cut my hair.

I knew that reading Frances' book did not make her my friend. But I was desperate to talk to someone who would sympathize with what I was going through. I found a phone number for the online shop where she sold her award-winning olive oil. I was ready to launch into an unbelievable set of reasons to explain why I needed to talk to this internationally bestselling author, when the most charming man answered the phone and told me that he would immediately pass me over to Frances. (I discovered later it was her husband, Ed.)

When she came on the line, I introduced myself and spilled out a rush of questions. She gently interrupted me and, in a delicious Southern drawl, asked, "Would you like to come and visit me?"

Would I? I must have been on her doorstep the next day!

Frances and I became friends and even now, long after my place was finished, she is still helping me to deal with the many dilemmas of living in Italy.

Please never ever be afraid to ask.

Admitting You're Bored Is the First Step

When I hear a woman announce that she's bored with life, my mother's voice rings in my head: "If you can't find something to do, I'll find you something." She always followed up with a list of dreaded chores.

"How can you be bored?" I once asked a stunningly beautiful forty-eight-year-old guest from New York. Her answer challenged me to rethink my impatience.

On the surface, Alice had a good life. After she married, she had given up her job as a stockbroker to stay home to raise two kids—she and her husband could afford it. Now that the kids were in college, she played tennis twice a week and was thinking of taking up golf. She had plenty of acquaintances and she wasn't isolated. But she had no intimate friends—no one she felt she could confide in about how empty her life felt. She was ashamed of her boredom and she told the group in Tuscany it was the first time she had been able to discuss it with anyone, including her husband. It turned out she was bored with him, too.

During her stay with us, Alice seemed to come alive. She laughed with the other women and she talked and talked. She chatted away on the hikes and she listened to other people's stories, their hopes and ideas for the future. She asked me endless questions about where I'd found the courage to start this next chapter in my own life. On the last morning, as eighteen sleepy, hungover women climbed into the vans for an early start to the Rome airport, Alice hugged me and whispered that she was leaving a different person than the one who had arrived a week earlier. "I am going home determined to find a meaning to my life," she said. "I don't care what it is but I have been inspired by you and everyone I have met here. I feel passionate about my next step even though I am not sure what it is."

Four weeks later, I received an email from Alice. She was just about to board a flight to Tanzania. She told me that on her journey home, she had begun to dream. By the time the plane touched down, she'd conceived a plan of action, determined to change her destiny. Her goal? To never allow herself to be bored again. She had to make this change for herself, she realized, because her marriage was over. Her kids were happy with their new student lives. While she would always be there for them, she wanted to be there for herself, too. Soon after she arrived back in New York, she contacted a humanitarian agency and volunteered to help build homes in Tanzania. She told me that through this journey to Africa she hoped to find her next chapter. A year later she was still there, living her dream.

My friend Donna has always struck me as the quintessential poster child of my "have-it-all/do-it-all" generation. She pursued a successful career in the marketing world, raised two fabulous kids and looked after her ailing in-laws as well as her own parents. At forty-nine, she decided to become a stay-at-home mom so she could take full advantage of the final precious years when her teenage daughters would be under her roof.

Within weeks of quitting her job, she was not only bored but actively hating not bringing in money she had earned herself. She had to get back out into the world, and she definitely wanted a salary, but for the first time ever, she realized she didn't have to be ruled by the size of the paycheque. She had the luxury of looking for something that she really loved.

One afternoon she wandered into a museum and took a tour. She was hooked, not only by what she learned about the artifacts but by the tour guide. When the crowd had dispersed, she chatted to the guide about her job and learned that there was actually a course that taught you how to be a museum guide. "Who knew?" she said when she told me, and laughed.

Donna jumped at the opportunity, took the class and now leads tours. When I spoke to her recently, she was on her way to Amsterdam to take part in a museum course there. How cool is that? Donna not only found a brand-new passion, but when her kids leave home, she's found an opportunity to grow in so many directions.

LESSON HOW TO SAY YES TO OPPORTUNITY

I am a firm believer in opening yourself up to new things. It's even more of a must when you are trying to discover your passion. The only way to meet opportunity full on is to get out there in the world. Yup, get off the couch and off your screens. Once you are out and about, I've found that one of the best ways to discover an opportunity is to do the complete opposite of what makes you comfortable.

I moved to Montreal at the tail end of my twenties. I loved the handsome young man I'd just married, but the transition to a new country made me lonely and miserable. After the first months of feeling sorry for myself, I finally realized that unless I started *living* in this new place, I would have to dump the love of my life

and go home to the UK. This was not an option I wanted
to entertain.

On a rainy May morning, I noticed a small poster
in the local Korean vegetable store advertising a fla-
menco dance class that was being held above the shop
that afternoon. I loved the flamboyant colours of the
dancer's outfit on the poster, but the idea of going to
a dance class filled me with horror. I like to dance but
only after several cocktails, and I display as much natural rhythm as a happy hippo. The thought of taking
dance lessons, sober and in the middle of the afternoon, made me cringe. But I also could not face another
empty day, so I bit the bullet and went to the class.

Then opportunity knocked: at the very first class,
I hit it off with the teacher and we became pals. Isabella
had recently moved from Barcelona to Montreal with
her sister. After the third lesson, when it was becoming
obvious that my dancing skills were and would remain
zero, she introduced me to her sister. Natalie was an artist who specialized in trompe l'oeil, creating images that
aim to trick the eye. She could transform a flat-fronted
standard door into a stunning antique wood-panelled
one that you had to touch to realize it was an illusion.
She was so talented she could even paint a person disappearing through the door.

I was thrilled at my luck in meeting her. I had
already begun to practise the art of faux paint finishes
on my own walls; I was getting expert at transforming
flat surfaces into aged parchment, faux marble and "dis-
tressed" plaster. We really enjoyed each other's company

and soon joined forces on decorating projects. For the next few years, we painted up a storm in homes, restaurants, clubs and even churches. If I had never walked into that dance class, I would never have found a partner to paint with. Eventually I was able to take my painting skills down a different route, thanks to the confidence I gained working with my talented friend.

Venturing outside your comfort zone can lead you into many unknown worlds. Dare to put your preferences aside and wander down the unexpected path: opportunity will reveal itself.

Off the Couch and Back into the World

I will never forget Liz, who told us her heartbreaking story on her very first evening in Tuscany.

After thirty happy years of marriage, Liz had been suddenly and unexpectedly widowed. The grief traumatized her so thoroughly it stunned her into immobility. She spent the three years after her husband died at home, rarely venturing out. "There was no point," she explained. "I basically lay on the sofa and watched television. My life felt heavy—my legs, my heart, even my mind was sluggish." Her married daughters were supportive and understanding, but they were also busy with their own families and unable to pull her out of her inertia. They pleaded with her to get out of the house but she remained stuck on that sofa.

The turning point came when a TV show sparked her interest. "I was watching Oprah's channel, not really paying much attention, when I heard your voice. There you were driving an old farm vehicle across the most beautiful landscape. I sat up and turned up the volume. As the credits rolled, I wiped away the tears and I called my daughter. I told her I wished to go to Italy to stay with Debbie Travis." (Liz had stumbled across *La Dolce Debbie*, my documentary about restoring the property and starting the Tuscan getaways.)

Her daughter said, "Mom, you've barely visited the supermarket and now you want to go to Italy?"

Liz had us all laughing, but she was serious as she told us that she got off that couch, sent us a registration form and six months later here she was in Tuscany.

I have rarely met anyone as determined as Liz. She told us she had never travelled abroad, even when she was married. This trip was as far out of her comfort zone as she could possibly leap. After her time with us, she spent the following two weeks exploring Rome on her own, though she was never alone for long. She found out that solo travelling was a perfect way to meet people. Even though she is still unsure of her new chapter, she has grabbed her life back from the hold grief had on it.

Seizing the Moment

When my sons were teenagers, we went on our first Caribbean family holiday. One of the highlights of the week was an afternoon spent parasailing. As the boat towed the parasail behind it, the kids happily soared, clinging tight while screeching with joy. I admit I only watched, comfortably safe in my spot on the boat, while chatting away with one of the owners of the outfit.

Even though she was in her mid-forties, Kathy looked like a fit, tanned American cheerleader. She told me she was originally from North Carolina and I asked her what had brought her to this beautiful place. Five years earlier, she'd been sitting exactly where I was now and her husband was the one who was up there flying through the air. They were tourists on a much-needed break from their stressful office jobs and their lives as parents—they had left their two small children with her mom and dad. While chatting to the previous owner, Kathy had confessed just how envious she was of her life running a parasailing business on the turquoise seas off the coast of the British Virgin Islands.

The owner told her that though she and her partner loved what they were doing, they were about to return to the United States to take care of her sick mother and were selling up. By the time Kathy's husband, Jim, had been unclipped from the sail and the boat had docked at the couple's hotel, the delighted four had shaken hands on a deal to buy the business, along with the owners' small house in town. To finance the deal, they sold their old home in North Carolina, then packed in their jobs, moved to the islands and registered the kids in the local school. Kathy and Jim knew themselves well enough to grab this chance at a different life in the space of an afternoon and went on to build a successful business in the Caribbean. Kathy said, "If we had thought too hard about it, I'm sure it would never have happened. It is the most impulsive thing we have ever done, but by far the very best."

Life can throw an opportunity at you when you are least expecting it. So be ready for it!

LESSON **FIND A SOUNDING BOARD**

"Women are each other's Wonderbra, supportive, uplifting, and making each other look bigger and better." I am not sure where I first heard this saying. Not only does it make me laugh, but I find it rings true.

We all need a friend and confidante. A person you can trust, who can be your sounding board as you share your passions and your dreams. I have had many close friends over the years, some of whom have boosted my confidence enormously when I've been starting a new project. Others, sadly, have been more like one of those ancient, overwashed, badly fitting bras with the bent wires than a Wonderbra. Years ago, when I produced and hosted the first episode of my first television series, I took the tape to a friend who lived nearby and sat in quiet trepidation as she watched. I admit I was hoping to be swamped with compliments. Instead, when the credits rolled, she turned to me and said, "Really, do you think anyone would be interested in watching a television show about decorating?" I felt like a deflated balloon.

I dragged myself home, and as I sobbed into my pillow, my youngest child said the obvious: "Mom, go and see another friend." Trust a child to see to the heart of things.

I took my little one's advice and carted my tape over to another neighbour's house. I watched her watching the episode and she could not shut up, constantly talking over the show. But she was saying things like, "Ooh, I could do that in my powder room." Or "Gosh, I love that—it would be great in my living room." Because of her unbridled enthusiasm, I knew I was on to something.

So find the right person to be your sounding board—someone you know is clear-eyed, but on your side. There is nothing so exhilarating as sharing ideas with a like-minded person. Eventually, in order to take the next step, you have to tell someone about the brilliant idea whirling around in your head. A friend's ear can help you make sense of your thoughts, and help you identify the positives along with the negatives.

I often become a sounding board for our guests in Tuscany. Recently, as we were on a magnificent hike through the olive groves, one of them asked me quietly if she could run an idea past me. Natasha Gargiulo was a well-known television entertainment reporter in her mid-thirties. She told me she found herself in a difficult place at the moment, but during her stay with me the fog had begun to lift and ideas were starting to surface. She asked me what I thought about her creating her own weekend getaways in a beautiful hotel owned by a friend in cottage country back home. By the time our hike was finished I was as excited by her idea as she was. Natasha now runs several homegrown retreats each year, inspiring and guiding other ambitious creative types. I am glad to have been the person she first confided in.

If It Makes You Happy

Helen, who lived two doors down from me in Montreal, has been my sounding board for decades. Picture an "Irish lass" and you'll see Helen, with her mop of flaming red hair, her charming lilt and wildly colourful way with the English language. She loved sharing a good bottle of wine or two with me on a Friday night as we bemoaned our busy, crazy lives. I was the best decorator on my street; she would be the first to admit she was the worst. I once asked her why she hung her very small, framed prints way up near the mouldings in her high-ceilinged Victorian townhouse. "Because that is where the **!^%** holes were when we moved in," she said. Clearly, our priorities were different.

Helen also happens to be one of the most brilliant women I know—a doctor, surgeon and researcher in the world of obstetrics. She was headhunted in Ireland by a US institution and eventually moved to Canada where she took a position at McGill University. We lived in such different worlds I have no clue how we became such good friends—probably the many bottles of wine on a Friday night! And, like me, she had two children and struggled daily with the constant juggling of family life and her stressful job. Like so many of us working moms, she was exhausted, physically and mentally. And it also turned out that she had a dream tucked away in the far reaches of that crackerjack mind.

She had studied medicine not so much for herself as to please her beloved father, and she had made him extremely proud. Then, seven years ago, he was killed in a tragic car crash. She was devastated and her mourning was intense. A year later, as she emerged from her grief, Helen told me at one of our one-on-ones that she was giving up the medical profession to follow her dream. "Ever since I was a child," she announced, hugging a glass of Pinot Grigio, "I have wanted to sing."

Helen is the farthest thing from impulsive. I knew—though it sounded totally out of left field—that if she had confessed this to me, she really *did* want to sing. I became her sounding board. I know nothing about the music business, but I was there to nod and smile and egg her on as she threw ideas at me. She did the planning and the homework, rearranged the finances, and made it happen. Her husband would take a job in Princeton, New Jersey, with a better salary so they didn't have to rely on her earnings. They would sell their home, move countries and buy a less expensive place to live, find a great school for the kids—all so she could follow her dream.

And she really did it. As soon as they were settled in New Jersey, she embarked on the long, arduous journey of singing lessons. Then she advertised for a band that she could join and found an incredible group of like-minded musicians. They now play at local events throughout the region, where they are hugely popular.

Helen was realistic and yet relentless in pursuing her dream. She had no ambition to win *American Idol* or become the next Beyoncé—she just wanted to sing. And sing she did—and does. She has just recorded her first CD, which is listed on iTunes. She also discovered she is a talented songwriter.

She is fifty-five now and she and her family have never been happier. Helen does not regret the many years she spent in medicine and the important work she did. As a doctor, she was fully aware of the incredible stress levels of her job, but it was the shock of her father's death that told her it was time to do something for herself: life is too short.

I am happy not only to be her friend but to have been her sounding board as she transformed her dream of being a singer into a thrilling next chapter.

DO IT

MY TEN COMMANDMENTS

Okay. You have dreamed up something fresh, something you feel passionate about. You could carry on dreaming forever, but that's not what this book is about. This is the moment to take the big chance on change. Of course, it is daunting to put yourself out there over something you care about. You can feel really vulnerable. But let's not put it off any longer: it's time to convert your dream and passion into action.

"But how?" I can hear you ask. "How do I actually do it?"

Over the past thirty years, I have started many new ventures—some that became hugely successful and some that were a disaster. If I had not had a set of my own rules to live and work by, I would probably have gone insane. These principles grew organically, without me even realizing I was creating a set of commandments that helped me juggle life as a working mother, start new projects and, most recently, dive into the unknown of a next chapter in Italy. I live by these rules and they have allowed me to become successful in my own next act.

I hope these commandments will help you gain the confidence and strength to travel down the different road you're imagining for yourself—or even make your current path a little easier to navigate.

COMMANDMENT 1

. . . .

LOSE THE FEAR

Fear of the unknown, fear of trying something new—fear of any form of change—is familiar to us all. Finding yourself at a crossroads can be mindnumbingly scary, but let's put *fear* into perspective.

Real fear can disable us, halt us in our tracks. It can also spur us into action. If you wandered into your backyard and were met by a roaring lion, you might freeze for a moment, but then the fear would propel you to leg it out of there before you got eaten! That's real fear.

Real fear is also that gut-wrenching physical dread that engulfs you when you have a seriously sick child. Or when you fall way behind on your rent or your mortgage and face losing your home. Or when a dark chill of emotion alerts you to the fact that your partner is having an affair and your relationship is probably over. Fear is having no control. If the bank is threatening foreclosure, fear will keep you up at night until you find a way to control the situation. You can help your sick child feel more comfortable, but his recovery is in the hands of the gods and in the hands of the doctors, not yours. You also can't control whether your partner will betray you. Fear on this level will overwhelm you for a while, but eventually it will be replaced by a slew of other emotions.

Fear is crippling. If we are ruled by our fears, we find it impossible to move forward. So let's not call the emotion you feel when you are challenging yourself to commit to a new chapter in your life *fear*. Let's describe it, instead, with more manageable words: you're anxious, you're worried, you're uncertain. That's nothing to be scared of! There is nothing truly *frightening* about taking a different path when your job feels like a constant Groundhog Day, or when being alone after a divorce or widowhood seems unbearable, or when you're rattling around an empty house after the kids have moved on. It would be more frightening for you in the long term to remain stuck in that place.

Instead, try to view your anxiety about change as totally normal. Remember that uncomfortable emotions help create the energy we need to change. We need to be cautious, of course, so make sure you stop to check that there are no obvious boulders in your way when you leap. But don't let your niggling worries stop you. If you're caught between a gut feeling that this move is really right for you and the fear that it all could go wrong, I recommend you always believe in your gut feeling.

For me, the best tool at this stage is pen and paper. The technique I suggested for finding your new dream is a good plan here too: write stuff down.

First, make a list of everything that is holding you back from creating your next chapter.

Second, make a list of everything you feel positive and excited about with regard to this new phase in your life. Lay the two lists side by side.

I can guarantee that at first your list of negatives will be very long and your list of positives quite short, even dinky. But take a hard look at those negatives, and start to differentiate between what is a true problem— something you have little or no control over—and what is an excuse.

"It's just not a good time" is an excuse. But "My husband is very sick" means it probably *is* the wrong time to embark on something new.

"I can't *afford* to make this happen" is a problem, but the kind of problem that likely has a solution. Start working on how you can solve that one, bit by bit.

As you cross out the excuses, your negative list will get shorter and your positive list will begin to grow.

To demonstrate the kind of list I'm recommending, I asked my sister-in-law to share her "fear" list. Though Sian has been divorced from my brother for over twelve years, we're very close and I adore my two nieces, Sian's daughters. One of them has just left for university in the UK, leaving her mother and sister behind in New York. Sian's other daughter will soon head out to her college of choice.

This is what Sian bravely tells me wakes her at the 3 a.m. witching hour:

- Fear of who I am apart from being an everyday mom. My daughters have been my main purpose in life. My focus, my drive, has been on their well-being and their futures. With them gone, I have lost my identity.

- Fear of living alone without family. Once the girls leave home, the closest family to me lives an ocean away in the UK.

- I am fearful that now I'm in my forties, I'm too old to start something new.

- I am afraid about money and security.

- What will motivate me to get through the day when I don't have to take care of my daughters?

- What will give me the kind of unconditional happiness I find with the children?

- Will life ever be full again?

- I am terrified of the unknown.

Every item on Sian's list is completely understandable. But let's try to put each one into perspective and think about how she can lose that fear. Which ones are unlikely to change because she has no control? Which of them, no matter how troubling they feel, are excuses?

Her angst about money and security is a problem, but she can potentially solve that one by seeking professional guidance to plan for her future.

The rest are normal vulnerabilities that she can banish by being more flexible about her circumstances.

She needs to make herself, not her daughters, the centre of her life now. Once she figures out how to do this, she will find out the world is still full of possibilities.

Sian is certainly not alone in worrying about what comes next after a significant passage of one's life is over. It took me a long time to adapt to the intense quiet in the house after both my sons had moved out. They do return often and the house immediately fills with their spirit, but it feels different now. Still, if you are awake to the possibilities, new doors always open.

Sometimes literally. After years of searching, Hans and I finally arrived at an ancient, wooden door fitted into an even older stone wall in the heart of Florence. We rang the rusty bell under the sign that declared that this was the office of Livio Garavaldi, notary at law. Thirty minutes later we walked out waving the deed to a pile of stone on a hundred-acre olive farm in the heart of Tuscany. We grinned at each other through lunch, smiled stupidly through our *aperitivi* and exulted more over dinner.

But later, at 3 a.m., that crazy hour of doubt, both of us were wide awake in bed in our musty B & B wondering what the heck we had done. At that godforsaken hour, our romantic move felt both stupid and overwhelming. But it was too late to back out—the money had been transferred to the former owners of the property and, for better or for worse, we were now the new proprietors.

RISING FROM ADVERSITY

ESTHER PILOTTI

I have known my friend Esther for many years. She comes from an Italian-Canadian family and a community where tradition lies deep—and no tradition is more honoured than caring for the elderly. Esther spent years going every day to look after her mother, who was widowed and living in the family home. But after her mother was diagnosed with Alzheimer's disease, Ester realized she needed full-time care. And Esther's own family needed her at home with them, not living full-time with her mother. Together they made a heart-wrenching decision: her mother would move to a care home. Then the nightmare began.

"I hated this time in my life," Esther told me. "Not because of my mother's condition, though that was emotional for us both. But what was truly difficult was finding a place that would take her." Esther found checking out facilities and gaining admission for her mother into the right one more challenging than choosing a good school for her son. Finally, after months of searching, they found a suitable home and moved her in. Her mother passed away just two years later. Esther was grief-stricken, but she was also angry over the suffering they'd all endured on the long search for the right place for her mother to end her days. Her anger transformed into a burning desire to do something.

After a few months of intensive research, Esther realized she and her family were not alone. There was a real need for an organization that would assist families to find the right care homes for their loved ones. Esther had just become an empty nester—her son was off to college and her husband worked long hours in the restaurant business. Why shouldn't she be the one to start the organization the community needed? "I had been looking for something for a while," she told me, "but I knew it had to be the type of work that would fulfill me. Even though the experience with my mother had no happy ending, I knew in my gut that the process of finding her a home should have been easier. Now I love the time I spend advising others who have found themselves in my shoes. It is not your normal kind of job, but it is humanizing. And it is so rewarding to witness the relief of everyone involved when we get it right."

I HAD
NO
CHOICE
BUT TO
CONQUER
THE FEAR

I will admit here that we were terrified on and off for the next few years. Even today, I still get stomach-lurching waves of "what have we done!"

The first time Hans "abandoned" me in Italy to go home and keep our business running, I stood forlornly in the muddy courtyard to wave him off. I felt lonely and pathetic and incompetent. Those feelings only got worse as I struggled daily trying to make myself understood by the builders. They were kind and skilled, and had renovated these types of medieval buildings numerous times before. I knew I was in good hands, but I was still scared. I had no choice but to conquer the fear, which meant doing my homework and trying to learn Italian while I took on the largest project of my life.

My two sons' straightforward advice always rebooted me when I was engulfed in doubt.

"You can do it, Mom," each of them told me. "You've tackled hundreds of decorating projects."

"Not like this," I grumbled. Transforming a hundred-acre estate on a hillside abroad is a far cry from redoing a guest bedroom in someone else's suburban house for a television show.

"You will be fine," they would say. "But can you hurry up? Because we want to bring some friends to stay."

Right.

Kids have the magic touch. They bring us back to reality with a laugh and help us conquer the fear.

I KNOW EXACTLY WHERE THEY'RE COMING FROM

DIETER RUYS AND CINDY VAN EECKHOUT

You sometimes meet the most extraordinary people in the most ordinary of places. I ran into Dieter and Cindy, a Belgian couple, in Spain while all three of us were having a drink in the same watering hole. I can't remember how we began to chat but we soon discovered we had some big things in common. I was already running my place in Tuscany, while they owned a B & B in one of the most stunning parts of Provence, in the South of France.

They told me that they had fallen in love while working alongside each other in Brussels at an IT company, as can happen, and married. Soon after their wedding, Dieter went on a business trip through Provence where he stayed in a series of small B & Bs that were either converted eighteenth-century farmhouses or beautiful villas. Because he was on his own, he often spent his evenings talking with his hosts, and he became intrigued with the lives they led. When he got back to Brussels, he took a deep breath and said to Cindy, "What if . . . ?" What if they packed in their jobs, bought an inexpensive property in the south of France, fixed it up themselves and opened their very own fabulous little hotel? Cindy said yes on the spot.

After they quit their jobs, they packed the car and drove to France. They spent only four days looking at properties (my search took ten years) and bought the fourth one they saw. The next few months were terrifying. First, they ran into serious problems with the transaction, but they were jobless and had to stick it out. They ended up moving in with the very old former owner and lived with him for two months in the run-down place until the paperwork was finalized. To generate some cash flow, they began booking rooms, but because of the problems with the sale, the two-thirds of a year they had estimated for renovations dwindled to five frantic months. But somehow they managed to restore the main building, build a pool, convert cow sheds into rooms and open in time—a miracle. That was sixteen years ago.

Dieter and Cindy's next chapter was life-changing. It was also extremely hard work. But now they and their two children are immersed in life in a tiny French village and have made many friends with guests from all over the world. They have no regrets about leaving their lucrative office jobs in Brussels. "There is no doubt it is challenging work at times and rarely glamorous," Dieter said. "But we love it—it is a magical life."

COMMANDMENT 2

....

I MEAN IT! DUMP THE EXCUSES

Who doesn't make excuses to get out of something you don't want to do, or to avoid taking the blame for a situation you're ashamed of?

The dog ate my homework.

No one will miss me if I don't go to the party because none of them really like me anyway.

There's no point in going to the gym today. I am way too fat.

If you have never made an excuse in order to stay under the covers on a rainy day, I am in awe of you.

But constantly making excuses for your shortcomings and failures to act is a serious matter. Excuses can cause you to avoid testing yourself on the real challenges of life. The person who actually suffers from such procrastination is you—no one else. Making excuses as to why you can't move forward will leave you with nothing but regrets for an unfulfilled life.

Here are some of the most common excuses for avoiding change and challenges, along with some effective ways to counteract them. Feel free to underline the ones that sound most familiar to you!

1.   **I am terrified of failure.**
     No one likes to fail, but if you spend time with any entrepreneur, he or she will often, almost giddily, tell you about the projects that did not

work out. Failure is part and parcel of who we are and how we grow. So take a moment to look back at some of the "failures" of your life. Do they seem that bad now? Really?

You won't be able to give your whole self over to a new adventure if you're too worried about failing. Believe, instead, that even if your plans don't work out, they will propel you into something else—they usually do. If you don't try because you're afraid of failure, you will never know what you missed.

2. **The future is so uncertain.**
The future scares all of us and it *is* unknowable. But your attitude is what will dictate how you experience the coming months or years. The best way to turn your fear and negativity into positivity is to work out how you would like to see your future unfold and then plan for it. Sometimes you need to dig deep to see what you are really afraid of; the answer may surprise you.

3. **I dream of change but I am afraid to try to make it happen.**
This excuse pops up when you're clinging to your comfort zone. You may feel intimidated because you lack experience or resources or simply have forgotten how to believe in yourself. Address your self-doubts with your confidantes. Don't set out to do the whole thing you're envisioning all at once; take small steps.

Encourage your body to be bolder by eating more healthily, joining a fitness club or going on daily walks. *Piano piano* as the Italians say— softly, softly: you don't have to change your whole life all at once. Foster your creativity by beginning a new hobby—anything that is a new experience can help build courage. Take up yoga, or baking, or painting, or salsa dancing. I know I've said you need to take a leap, but there is no need for you to jump into your big project of transformation head first. If you take small, manageable steps, bit by bit your fear of change will evaporate.

4. **I can't afford it.**
    So you have an innovative idea but are worried about financing this dream. A perfectly legitimate worry. But don't allow it to become an excuse. Find professional help and advice from people who have been there and done that to craft a strategy to reach your monetary objectives. (And see the section on budgeting later in this book.)

5. **I am too old (or too young) for a new project.**
    You are never too old or too young. Spend an evening googling what others have achieved no matter the numbers of birthdays they've had: there really are no limits. Find the positives in your age. If you are middle-aged, dwell on the fact that you now have the freedom to

do things that were just not possible when you were in the thick of establishing that first career. Realize that you bring a lifetime of experience to the table. Think of the contacts you have made over the years and how to explore that address book of yours. Think of what you already know about the world and about how things get done.

If you're young, don't let your youth or lack of experience hold you back from a compelling adventure. Educate yourself. Ask for advice, learn the ropes, make it happen. Sometimes you'll find a way simply because you don't know the "old ways" of doing things. Take advantage of the enviable fact that you have youth on your side.

6. **I've got no training for this.**
That really *is* an excuse. My grandmother went to college when she was seventy-five to finish her high-school education, which had been cut short by the Second World War. She was the oldest in her class by decades and she loved it. In fact, she graduated high school and remained in college taking more courses until she died ten years later.

What you don't know, you can learn. I had no qualifications to become a designer, but I did. TV host? I learned on the job. Businesswoman and CEO of my company? Learned by my mistakes. Writer? Well, you be the judge. Retailer? Figured it out as I went along. Hotelier? I'm still winging it. Some very successful people did not rely on higher education and lining up the right credentials to get where they wanted to go. Here's a brief list of the self-taught, just as they come to mind: Anna Wintour, Ellen Degeneres, Ted Turner, Steve Jobs, Rachel Ray, Richard Branson, Simon Cowell, Michael J. Fox, Ringo Starr, Maya Angelou, Lady Gaga and Winston Churchill. I could go on.

The point is, what you don't know you can learn in numerous ways. Sure, go back to school if that's the best path to your destination, or take night courses, offer to shadow someone on the job, take every opportunity to ask questions of people who are where you long to be.

I'm often asked how I became a television producer. If I'd been deterred by a lack of training, I never would have become one. It all began when I was a model, working on a commercial shoot in Holland. There were eight of us there, all frightfully bored as we sat around waiting for our turn in front of the camera. My eyes were constantly drawn to a stunning older woman (she was probably only in her late twenties, but that seemed ancient to me at the time) who was running around the set with a yellow clipboard giving animated instructions to the crew. She looked so in charge, so bossy . . . and that was right up my alley. I asked someone what her role was, and they said she was the producer.

I asked someone else, "So how do you become a television producer? Actually, what is a television producer?"

The advice that changed my life? "Hang around the pubs where the TV people drink and you'll soon meet someone who can get you a foot in the door."

I did, and it worked. The person I met told me to get on a course at the BBC, which would be a step towards an internship. I spotted an evening class in set design for TV and film that was just about to begin, and signed up. When I showed up, though, everyone in the room seemed at least twenty years older than I was, and all of them had credentials as architects or engineers. They had compasses, protractors and other smart tools of the design trade with them, whereas I had a pencil and a plastic ruler. I fled from class, miserably embarrassed, and took refuge in the BBC canteen, where I encountered a kind woman who actually happened to be a producer. She asked me what was wrong, and I told her what had happened, and she said, "Hang on a sec, I'll be right back." When she returned, she handed me an application for an internship at the BBC. She'd written her name across the top and beside it the thrilling word "Recommended." Two weeks later, I was in.

And, yes, I got myself a yellow clipboard.

7.   **It's just not the right time.**

But what is the right time? If you wait around for the perfect moment, I guarantee it will never come. We all have the same twenty-four hours in a day. How you use those hours is up to you. Putting things off is easy. So ask yourself how badly you want this to happen. Plan and plot. Chop up what you need to do into achievable pieces. Then make a schedule, set deadlines and get each of those pieces done. Give yourself a year, if you need it.

8.   **What if people laugh at me?**

Ditch this excuse as fast as you can. Life is too short to spend time worrying about what others think of you. Most of the people you assume are judging you are wondering about how they are doing in their own lives, not giggling behind your back about what you are trying to do with yours. More people are wishing you well than thinking you are ridiculous or doomed to failure—no matter what Twitter has to say. Share your hopes and dreams with friends. Some of them will not know how to react, because that's just human nature. But you will be pleasantly surprised by most of them.

Everyone struggles to begin with; everyone is undermined at some point or other by uncertainty, self-doubt and fear. We are all in the same boat, so don't use this as an excuse not to set sail.

COMMANDMENT 3

. . . .

GET UNSTUCK

We have to stop clinging to the shirttails of our past lives. We need to move on in our heads and, also, emotionally. We need to let go of that spouse we divorced and the routines and priorities of our lives as parents. We need to look past the job that has never felt right and find one that stimulates us. Memories are part of who we are, but when you embark on a new phase in your life, you need to be thinking forward not looking back.

To help unstick yourself from your old ways, try this exercise suggested by Lucy, the life coach who works with the women at our retreats. Write two separate letters to yourself, one about your past and the other about your future.

The first letter can be a simple list of your accomplishments so far: finishing university (or not, in my case!), meeting your partner, having your kids, milestones with friends, meaningful travels, landing your first big job. Describe what the previous years have meant to you. Include the good, the bad and (never forget) the ugly.

Devote real time to this letter to yourself, even if you end up scribbling away while sobbing into a large gin and tonic. I've been there, and I know that your emotions will range from pure joy and gratitude to sadness and even anger. Get it all down. When it's done, read it through, and if you cry again, that's fine. Cry happy tears and cry tears of pain. Cry for your losses and the wrong steps you took. Then bury that letter somewhere.

Now write a second letter—to your future self. Jot down what you would like to accomplish, your dreams, and your passions. Be in a positive frame of mind when you do this and spontaneously write what comes to you. Describe how dearly you want this next phase to happen—whether it's a new job, a new business, a new country you want to explore, a new way to make a difference by helping others. Outline the commitment you promise to make to achieving this future. Mention your goals and the mindset you intend to be in for this next chapter.

Don't bury this letter. Keep it handy. Read it frequently. When you feel at a loss or adrift or overwhelmed, read it again to remind yourself of the journey you've promised yourself to take.

I began my next chapter by hosting a single retreat a year in a place we had to rent. But when our renovation of the property we'd bought was finished, and eighteen rooms were waiting to be filled every second week for several months, it was obvious I was going to be really busy—so busy I was in danger of losing the family-and-friends time that had made me cry in the Thai sauna. I was so worried, Lucy the life coach suggested I write a "future letter" to myself.

It was hard. One of the aspects I found completely daunting was straddling two different worlds. I tingled with the thrill of opening the Tuscan property to guests, and sharing a little of the *dolce vita* with people from many countries and walks of life. Yet I was not (and I still am not) ready to break ties with my business life back in Canada. When I wrote down where I would like to be with the retreats in a few years, I also added plans for new television series, a new home product line, a wine collection and, yes, a book I would write (this one) about next chapters.

My letter to myself was rather long. And it was a massive wake-up call. Yikes, my plate was full. But because I'd got it all down on paper, I could clearly see that I needed to plan my time well and that I needed help. As a result, I was able to figure out a way forward. Instead of burning myself out, I decided to offer a couple of our loyal and talented long-time employees partnerships in the business. With that one move, I not only gave to those employees a chance to become owners of something they loved, I freed both Hans and myself to spend more time on the retreats, with each other and with our friends and family.

It can be hard to untangle ourselves from the old ways of doing things, those deeply ingrained habits. But life is full of many chapters, and if you want to move on successfully, it is imperative to make a conscious effort to shed the past and embrace what comes next. Then the fun can begin.

WHEN OPPORTUNITY SLAMS INTO YOU

SANDRINE DE MONTPLAISIR

After twenty-five years of living in Paris, Sandrine, a lawyer, and her husband, Daniel, who worked for France's National Assembly, were bone-tired of the city and their professional lives there. Sounds crazy, right? Most of us would give our eye teeth to live in the City of Light, at least for a while. The couple idly dreamed of a new culture and new life, but they didn't take any steps to deal with their dissatisfaction with the status quo until their teenaged daughter came back from a visit to Montreal as an exchange student. She raved about her experience and her fascination with Montreal endlessly, and told her parents that one day she was going to attend McGill University there. As Sandrine and Daniel patiently listened to their daughter, they found themselves increasingly caught up in her excitement about this Canadian city far away across the Atlantic.

Then Daniel admitted that he thought he had reached as high as he would go in the French government and confided that he would like to pursue his calling as a historian. Sandrine was also ready for a change in her career, but she found the idea of moving to another country overwhelming. "We flip-flopped endlessly, trying to make a decision," she told me. "At times the idea seemed so exciting and at others preposterous. But the more we talked to friends and shared the vision, the more solid the idea became. When I think back, we could have gone on discussing the move forever. But then the phone rang. It was a French publishing house that wanted Daniel to write a book about the history of Canada."

An opportunity had slammed into them and now all they had to do was grab it. Within three months, the family had sold their apartment in Paris, found a school for their daughter and a house in Montreal. Newly settled in Quebec, Sandrine was filled with energy to pursue ambitions she had never had the nerve to dream of in France. It took her several years, but she successfully created Sydencanne, an amateur film festival in Montreal, and is working on a play about immigration. Daniel finished his book and now writes for several magazines. And just as she had dreamed, their daughter is a student at McGill.

COMMANDMENT 4

....

TAKE THE RIGHT AMOUNT OF RISK

I have never smoked, never gambled and rarely taken drugs, not for any sanctimonious reason but just because none of these have ever been my kind of thrill. What does give me goosebumps is the thought of a good risk. I thrive on that heady sense of moving forward into uncharted territory. I love pitting my logic, intelligence and perseverance against a challenge, especially when I'm not certain I can pull it off. Of course, being free to take a risk is related to being able to make a choice at all. These days, choice is less of a rarity than it was for the generations of women who came before me.

My mother's generation seemed to have little say over the options life had to offer women. (I'm thinking of you, Mrs. Ramsbottom.) My mother did pick my father, thank heavens, though there are still countries and cultures where that basic choice is not an option. But she had no choice about whether she would take on the domestic duties of housework and child-rearing. Dad had the job in the family, and in our part of the world, there were no nannies or day care or even after-school programmes to give Mom more possibilities than just staying home. After my father died, she had no choice about how she would pay the bills: with young kids at home, she couldn't go out to work, so she took in lodgers.

I still remember an Easter holiday in my early twenties when I'd gone home for a family get-together and my siblings swarmed me as soon as I walked in to tell me that Mom had got a job. It turned out that, in secret, she had done the training in order to qualify as a masseuse, had bought herself a special table and set up shop in the dining room. As the supportive children we were, we all rolled around laughing, and when we got serious it was to push her guilt buttons: "What about us?" (Two of us had already left home, and the others were finishing high school: What were we thinking?)

She ignored us, and when the doorbell rang at six o'clock, she calmly picked up a pile of neatly folded towels and her bottle of massage oil and went to let her client in.

What a risk-taker! She loved her new job, and kept on giving massages to friends and neighbours until she was too sick to stand. Two years later, at fifty-four, she died of cancer, but not before she'd jumped thoroughly out of her comfort zone.

Nothing can be achieved without taking a risk. But you need to decide how much risk you can bear. Successful risk-taking is all about calculating the risk—weighing what is at stake. While I've argued (and will argue again) that failure is your friend, I'm not talking about setting yourself up for a *crushing* flop. You need to think through how much time, effort and money you are capable of investing in a new venture, and risk just that.

People of different ages have different perspectives on risk. A young person may worry that taking time out to pursue a new venture means missing a rung or two on the career ladder. But maybe, even if you fail, you'll come back to that old career with a new experience that expands your portfolio. I've hired staff for over twenty-five years, and I've never been particularly interested in where someone went to school, their academic record or their qualifications on paper. I look for the bold and courageous ones who have tried new things, whether they succeeded or fell on their faces. I want the hard workers who join our production company to have life experience.

If you're older, often you have more time to invest in a new venture, along with maturity of judgment. You also have your savings and perhaps a home to use as collateral. But as the successful senior entrepreneur Tricia Cusden advises, if you have $40,000 in the bank, don't invest it all in your new idea. If you fail, and lose it all, you'll have much less time to earn it back. You need to figure out the amount you can afford to lose, and risk only that.

What you will also risk is disappointment. It's rare that a new venture works a hundred percent as planned. The thought of failing should never hold you back, since failure is how projects are perfected. But you also need to protect your assets so you can bounce back and try something else.

I doubt you remember a series called *Completely Hammered* (my husband's title, not mine). The concept was fun. Three hunky men, half-naked most of the time because we filmed in the sweltering summer months, would visit women's homes and help them with odd jobs—broken door handles, tiling a wall, laying a floor—anything that also could be pitched as instructional. In reality, the show was nauseating. There was too much innuendo. Typically, the host would smirk and say something like "Oh, just stick it in the hole," as the woman homeowner popped a screw into the wall. Deservedly, it bombed. But it didn't take any of our other shows with it because, as was our practice, we'd made the series its own separate production company.

We'd taken a risk on the three cute guys with skills, and failed. But something good still came out of it: there was value in the idea of a show about a man who was handy with tools. Our next launch was called *Income Property*, and it was hosted by a handsome fellow named Scott McGillivray, who first had joined us on the HGTV series *Debbie Travis' Facelift*. He was likeable and talented—and the camera loved him. By taking a risk on a show that flopped, we found the seeds of another show that became a big success.

So take a risk. If you don't take a flyer, you'll never know what could have been. As Eleanor Roosevelt said, "You must do the thing you think you cannot do." Or, as an aphorism that bounces around social media goes, "Do one thing every day that scares you."

COMMANDMENT 5

....

BE MINDFUL OF YOUR MINDSET

I really take to heart a wonderful aphorism from Dr. Wayne Dyer (an author and thinker who's been called "the father of motivation"): "If you change the way you look at things, the things you look at change."

If you are standing at that crossroads debating what is next for you, it may take more than having a new idea to get you going. You may need to change your mindset. Let's say you've decided you need to become a corporate refugee in order to follow your dream of opening a gorgeous bed and breakfast in the countryside. This new chapter is going to be very different from the last, so *you* need to be different too. Old habits must be broken and new ones developed. For a new role you may need to be a new you.

How true. For twenty years, I had my hair blow-dried nearly every morning in my kitchen by Danny the hairdresser while the kids ate breakfast. Then I had my makeup applied. A stylist brought my clothes for the day. I had full-time assistants. When I came home at night, I was just Mom and got the dinner ready, but I never really thought about how good I had it.

Now, in Italy, while the retreats are running, you'll often see me dashing across the courtyard with fresh towels or a hair straightener for a guest who has an urgent need. I admit it did take me a while to change my mindset and not get upset when a guest would casually ask me to bring them another glass of chilled white wine. *Me??* But really, who else would they ask but their host?

Often our desire to make a change actually springs from the simple longing to be in a different headspace. We have the sinking feeling that we can't change the way we think or respond; sometimes we feel we've been typecast since we were kids, and there's no use fighting it. *Johnny is a good cook. Moira is the funny one. Jane is great at parties.* But I've always believed that having a talent for something is only a small part of the equation. I made my name designing the interiors of homes for television shows, but that is not my talent. Yes, I have a good eye, but I am not a great designer. To make the best shows I hired creative people to help me. I knew what I wanted, but I needed to put a team together to make it happen. So don't get stuck thinking you don't have what it takes. If you are craving something different, start thinking about what you need to make that happen.

Our minds are constantly monitoring where we are. Unhappiness, frustration and too much stress can exaggerate everyday emotions so that a situation makes us angrier or sadder than it should. The wrong mindset has us constantly judging ourselves and the people around us—and deciding that we are all wanting. A good mindset is open to opportunity, personal growth, new ventures and even criticism, and is able to roll with the ups and downs.

FROM THE CORPORATE WORLD TO MAKING KNICKERS

JOANNA GRIFFITHS

I worked with Joanna Griffiths at the television network that aired my series *All for One*. We clicked but lost touch after the show was finished airing. Next time I heard something about Joanna, I couldn't believe the twist that had happened in her life story. So I got in touch and over coffee she told me about her fascinating adventure.

One day some years ago, she was chatting with her mom—a doctor and a mother of four—about the physical realities of being a woman and the changes that can happen in different life stages. Joanna was only in her mid-twenties at the time, and some of the issues her mom was telling her about were not exactly on her radar. For instance: "My mom told me how one in three women leak when they laugh, dance, sneeze or do jumping jacks."

Joanna had always believed her ambition was to become the CEO of an entertainment company. To further her career, she took a year off work and travelled to France to study for an MBA with the intention of then landing the big dream job. But something changed her while she was in France. She relaxed, enjoying the pace of life, and her mind began to wander. And her thoughts constantly cycled back to her conversation with her mother.

Soon she was talking to every woman she met about underwear. The more forthcoming the women were, the more personal the questions Joanna asked. As the months passed, a strong picture began to emerge: women of all ages, leaks or no leaks, wanted underclothes that were beautiful, practical and comfortable. "I became obsessed with underwear," Joanna said.

When her year in France was over—during which she had interviewed hundreds of women—she returned to Canada feeling compelled to reinvent the structure of women's underwear. Even though she had job offers from major media companies in Los Angeles and Europe, her ambitions had changed radically. "Instead, I began my company, which I called Knix. I worked on one piece at a time, from leak-proof underwear to wire-free bras. Now the collection includes tanks, T-shirts, lounge wear, sports bras and a teen line called Knixteen that encourages young girls to be the boss of their periods."

The first three years were incredibly hard. "I was newly married and we used the money we had saved up to buy a house to invest in the underwear company," Joanna said. "It was a risk. The first couple of years I didn't make any money and I worked around the clock. The hardest part, though, was when the company started to do well! My mindset was in the wrong place. I was hard on myself, feeling like I didn't deserve the success. I was unintentionally holding myself back."

Even though she was driven, she knew there was something wrong with the way she thought about herself. In the fall of 2016, Joanna attended a conference called Summit at Sea that brought together entrepreneurs, activists, artists and investors on a multi-day cruise in the Bahamas. "Over the course of that cruise, I decided I was going to change my mindset and in doing so change my life. I needed to stop competing with others and start celebrating what I had already achieved. Instead of thinking 'No, not me,' I started saying 'Why not me?'"

When she got home to the business, everything changed. "Since then our sales have grown over 2000 percent and a Knix item is sold every ten seconds," she told me. "Each day I feel a connection to the women that we serve. Every day I know we make a difference in how women feel about their bodies. Every day I feel challenged. Now I couldn't imagine doing anything else."

Our minds are our best friends and worst enemies. We easily jump to the most negative conclusions, and that only holds us back. How often do you assume that if you don't hear back from someone after reaching out on email that the person is either not interested or deliberately ignoring you. That was me, until I gave myself and others a break by deciding to assume instead: "Technology isn't perfect. Maybe that email went to junk mail or was lost in the ether." "Maybe she was on a deadline, and just forgot to get back to me." Instead of being negative and defeatist, adopt a mindset that assumes the best, not the worst.

Build a personal toolbox that you can dip into when negativity raises its ugly head. One friend of mine, a successful businesswoman, goes for a run when nasty, defeatist thoughts take over her mind, and she says each of these thoughts out loud as she runs. She told me she always feels better afterwards, as if she sent these worries off into a universe far far away from her. When I start hearing "What's the point, just give up" running through my head, I allow myself to take *one* mopey day at home on the couch in my pyjamas. I watch a soppy movie on TV and wallow a bit. By the end of the day, I find I can put all those thoughts back into the box where they belong and forget about them. You need to find ways that work for you.

I have known my friend Sandra for decades, and we often share stories of our lives in long phone calls. Recently, she'd been through a tough time—she'd just been divorced, she missed her grown-up kids, and she was at a low point in a job she'd been in for ten years. But I hadn't realized how negative her state of mind was until one day she announced to me over the phone, "I have had it. I am tired of being angry all the time, fed up with being sad, and I am bored at work. I don't like 'me' very much so how can I expect others to like me."

Sandra knew it was time for a change, and she also knew that the first step was to change her mindset. She used her version of the box technique and packed the undermining thoughts in there, locked the box and threw away the key. Two months later, she called to tell me she had quit her job and was taking a nutrition course where she was meeting all kinds of new and interesting people who shared her interests. Money was tight, so she had decided to sell the family home and buy a condo. She removed all the obstacles getting in the way of her exciting new life bit by bit, until she'd banished her negativity.

COMMANDMENT 6

....

EMBRACE YOUR MISTAKES

We live in a world where we feel ashamed when we get things wrong. But I've learned, as have lots of other people who make it a habit to try, try and try again, that it is not making the mistake that is the problem, but our fear of making a mistake. How can we move forward when we think we need to be perfect? Isn't it simply deluded to think we should never make a mistake?

Mistakes are par for the course. I have made too many to count. I've found that inventing a solution to deal with one of my screw-ups is actually a creative endeavour that leads to more creativity. You goof, and then you bounce in a direction that you might never have thought of if you hadn't made that wrong call. For each and every problem, there is a solution, and you learn something every time from the attempt to find that solution.

Mistakes open us up to opportunity. They lead us towards another path. Mistakes we make on this journey of next chapters are part of a pilgrimage to a place that brings us joy. And challenges, too, of course. But these are challenges you can look forward to conquering.

I firmly believe in nothing ventured, nothing gained. I embrace my mistakes because they are part of me and part of what I have built. When I look back, I can see why I made all my wrong turns. It may be painful to stumble, but get up, put a bandage on that mistake, let it heal and use what you've learned to grow.

You are likely thinking that I'm sounding pretty abstract here. So I'll give you a concrete example. In my twenties, I worked as an assistant film editor in the edit suite of a newsroom at one of the small regional TV channels in the UK. Every day we lowly types would hang around waiting for the mad rush when the news footage would arrive. We would then jump into action to assist the editor in cutting the six-o'clock news line-up.

The editor I was assisting would do his waiting in the pub across the street. One afternoon after the footage of our piece—a helicopter rescue—had arrived, I dashed over to get him and found him slumped over his fourth pint of beer. There was no rousing him. I went back to the editing suite, where I stared in panic at the rolls of 16mm film (no digital in those days). I took a deep breath and jumped into action. I would edit the piece myself. I cut and spliced and put the story together from the producer's notes. I delivered the three-minute item just in time to air and then galloped home.

When I got back to my flat, I turned on the news. There was my story, but the footage of the helicopter was upside down.

The next morning I was fired. I had been unafraid to make a mistake but I lost my job over it.

Two weeks later, another editor at the station contacted me. He was going freelance in order to make a documentary in Africa. He told me he loved my spirit. Would I like to work for him? I took the job, and what an experience that turned out to be. He launched his documentary at the Cannes television festival in the south of France and he invited me to come to the premiere. The cherry on the cake is that Cannes is where I met my future husband.

Please, embrace your mistakes. Look where mine led me.

COMMANDMENT 7

....

HANG ON TO YOUR SENSE OF HUMOUR

When you grow up in the UK, you need a sense of humour to fend off the drizzle that can steadily fall on this brilliantly green island. Having a good laugh is imperative or the grey skies will drown you in gloominess. Conversations, however serious, usually end in a joke and a giggle.

We all know people with absolutely no sense of humour. Thank God they are rare. Most of us understand how humour diffuses the dramas of our daily lives. Take a toddler who falls over and begins to wail. If his mother rushes to him looking frantic, the noise escalates. But if she laughs and acts out the "bump" like a clown, the crying inevitably turns to chortling.

Crappy stuff happens but humour changes the context and mitigates the impact, turning a disaster into a funny story you eventually can share with a friend. I find nothing more pleasurable than making other people laugh, even when it's at my own expense. Here's one story that still makes me turn pink. Actually, it's so embarrassing it makes me want to crawl under a rock and hide. But it also makes people laugh, so here goes.

Many years ago, while I was still living in Montreal, I was asked to host a live weekly decorating segment on a morning television show for the CBC. Great! So every week, I'd pack everything I needed for whatever project or decorating technique I was going to demonstrate into my car and make the long drive to Toronto, do my bit and drive home. On one of these occasions, I'd just got to the studio and was unpacking my gear onto a table in the green room—only vaguely conscious of the elegant, elderly man sitting quietly on the oversized sofa across from me. Soon I was interrupted by a spotty youth with a clipboard who asked which one of us was Debbie Travis. Snarkily, I didn't respond, given that it was totally obvious since I was the only woman in the room. But the gentleman on the sofa smiled kindly and pointed towards me. The youth swivelled my way and announced, "I am sorry, Ms. Travis, but your segment has been cancelled because we're devoting the whole show to Mr. Mandela."

In a real snit, I began slamming my decorating tools back into my carrying case, and think I may have even muttered, "Seriously?!" The old man got up off the couch and came over to me to tell me how sorry he was that I'd been treated this way and to inquire what I had been about to talk about on the show. I grumpily replied, "I was about to show people how to strip off wallpaper. And you?"

"World peace," said Nelson Mandela. Because that's who this thoughtful man was—the statesman who brought South Africa out of the apartheid era, who'd been incarcerated for decades on Robben Island and was currently his country's head of state.

I left Toronto feeling so ashamed I wanted to die: How had I not immediately recognized him? But by the time I was a couple of hours from home, I started to giggle.

Wallpaper removal or world peace? Hmnn, so which one of those was more important?

It was an excellent lesson on the importance of not taking yourself too seriously.

However life-changing your new chapter might be, it won't stop the world going round if you fall flat. The disasters that inevitably result from embarking on something new may not seem so hilarious when they first happen. But, if you learn from such experiences and put them in perspective, most of them soon will.

Another case in point (and I have many more where this came from). Even when I have no talent for something, I always have ideas and the entrepreneurial spirit to go for it. As I've mentioned, when my best friend, Jacky, and I were young, we were models in London. Models, I stress—not supermodels earning fortunes. We were always looking for ways to supplement our incomes and fill the hours between jobs.

We were in love with the clothes of Norma Kamali, an iconic American fashion designer who was a pioneer in the shoulder-pad revolution. One afternoon, when we were wandering around her boutique on a hip London street, we each dared to try on one of her long suede skirts. We were crazy about them. We pranced around the changing room, knowing full well that there was no way in our wildest dreams we could afford them.

On the bus home, I told Jacky that while the Norma Kamali skirts were awesome, I thought they looked pretty easy to make. I hatched a plan: we would buy lengths of suede in beautiful colours and sew them ourselves, then sell them to all our friends. By the time we disembarked the no. 44 bus, in our own minds we were already wealthy fashion designers.

We enticed a couple of girlfriends to pay for their skirts up front, then found a cheap tannery and bought ten pieces of suede in electric colours. Sadly, neither of us could sew. Worse, working with suede is definitely not for beginners. But that is why they invented the glue gun.

We cut the suede into large strips on the bias and used our newly purchased device to hot-glue them together. Not so stupid, you are thinking.

We delivered skirts to our two friends, put on our own, and the four of us danced the night away in a sweaty disco. Until the glue began to melt. The skirts fell apart on the dance floor, leaving us wearing only the waistbands.

I admit it took us a while to see the humour in our humiliation. In the meantime I became smitten with the glue gun and threw myself into numerous craft projects. We rented a market stall and on the weekends sold everything we made with that precious gun.

Jacky and I now share this story and others with our guests in Italy to help them gain "perspective," sure, but also for the simple reason that they make us laugh. Nothing seems quite so bad when you can laugh about it, even when you're standing in your knickers on a dance floor with a pool of suede at your feet.

COMMANDMENT 8

. . . .

GET CONNECTED

I hate to date myself but I do scratch my head wondering how Hans and I ever managed to run our businesses without social media. How on earth did we get a new TV series off the ground or a new product selling in the stores? Good old word of mouth, I suppose, along with a mass of expensive advertising. The tools we have today make starting a fresh chapter a dream. You can run a business from your kitchen table, learning from others already active in the area you're interested in—tackling your research without even leaving home.

But for our own sanity we need to pause and consider the meaning of the word "social." Look it up on Merriam-Webster.com and you'll see it described as "relating to or involving activities in which people spend time talking to each other or doing enjoyable things with each other: liking to be with and talk to people: happy to be with people: of or relating to people or society in general." As in liking to be face to face with real people in real time and in the flesh.

The many forms of social media offer us endless support and affirmation of our points of view, and an abundance of ways to reach out around the globe. But there is nothing quite like the sound and feel of real, live, human connection. And nothing so inspirational, either.

Two years ago, I took a flight as part of a long publicity trip across North America in support of a new product line. Everyone around me on the plane was glued to their personal screens. Then the gentleman sitting next to me said hello to the flight attendant who had brought him a glass of wine, and turned and said hello to me too. Instead of returning to his iPad, he engaged me in conversation. By the time we landed, I had registered him and his wife (a surprise Christmas present) for my first couples' gourmet retreat (his idea). He was on the cusp of retiring and our long chat had also inspired him to start another business. So in the course of this flight, I had made a new friend and started a gourmet retreat for couples; and he too had a new idea for his next chapter. None of this would have happened if we'd both spent the flight on our devices.

Engaging with real people does take more effort than pounding away on a laptop, but it is imperative that we don't lose this God-given skill or the desire to embrace a face-to-face conversation. It may lead to something interesting, but you will never find out what that fascinating thing might be unless you open yourself to the people you meet.

A couple of years ago I was the keynote speaker at a luncheon in which most of the fifty tables had been bought by companies for their employees. I was five minutes into my speech when I stopped and asked the audience if they were all there, primarily, to network. When I saw lots of nods around the room, I asked why they were all sitting at tables with colleagues they saw every day. Then I asked everyone to stand up and switch to a table where they didn't know anyone (as you may have gathered, I am rather bossy). At first they all seemed to freeze in horror, but then the whole room started to move. After the hubbub died down, I carried on with my speech. By the time I climbed down from the stage, everyone was mingling beautifully, and many people came up to tell me what a great idea it had been to shift them all around. To me it was just common sense, but still it gave me a thrill to see all the cards and even hugs exchanged at the end of that lunch.

One of my favourite ways to get a conversation going is to take a walk with someone. We take daily hikes with our guests in Italy, partly because we need to burn the calories from the wonderful meals, but also because there is nothing more exhilarating and conversation-enhancing than strolling through the Tuscan countryside. Literally putting one foot in front of another can free you to see the next steps of your own journey.

At a hiking spa I once visited in northern California, I met fourteen strangers who, like me, thrive on good long walks. I made some firm friends during that trip, one of them a retired woman in her sixties who was feeling bored. On the trail, she shared her story with me. Her husband was still working, so she was alone much of the time. She now regretted retiring because she felt she had more to give to the world. During the last mile, as I panted away, she gushed about how she lived for chatty hikes like this. By the time we were unlacing our boots she was full of excitement about her new idea: she was going to go home and launch a hiking club. The idea had to have been squirrelled away in her brain somewhere, but our long talk while we walked pulled it to the surface. She followed through, and now she delights in taking people on hikes in far-flung places around the world. She could have come up with this idea while googling away in her living room, but I like to think it was the fresh air and my company that gave her that aha! moment.

I recently read an article in the *Harvard Business Review* titled "4 Steps to Having More 'Aha' Moments," by David Rock and Josh Davis, that explains why light-bulb moments often happen when you're as relaxed as we were on that hike. The two write that going directly at a problem or a quest for inspiration is maybe not the right way to go about it. Creative insights and solutions to problems tend to "pop" into our brains when the mind is relaxed and running free. They recommend turning your devices off and unplugging from your obligations for a few hours at a stretch, several times a week, because ideas tend to come to you when you aren't looking for them.

I have ideas constantly when I am driving, and I often have to pull over and jot them down. I believe that many ideas are already there, running around inside your head, but they need a relaxed mind to show themselves.

COMMANDMENT 9

. . . .

NEVER CURB YOUR ENTHUSIASM!

Excitement is a good feeling. An amazing feeling.

You likely know people who are constantly enthusiastic and thrilled by whatever they are embarking on. Their passion is contagious: we want to be around it, even grab a part of it for ourselves.

It is impossible to jump into a new chapter if you're feeling down. Excitement about what's around the next bend drives us forward and opens us up not only to the next opportunity but to finding ways to seize hold of it. No one wants to listen to a pitch for an idea from someone who isn't excited. We need to believe in our new venture enough to shout it from the rooftops.

I don't mean that you suddenly have to become a loud and noisy extrovert: I can't tell you how nervous I get when I have to stand up in front of people and pitch them on a new idea. You just need to be so in love with your new venture you can't help but communicate that love.

Hans, who is my rock through the constantly evolving chaos of my life, was with me every step of the way through the renovation of Villa Reniella and the launch of the retreats, and he also still runs our production company. A few years ago I was nodding off during a long flight with my head tucked into my favourite spot on Hans' shoulder when he mumbled something about turning fifty, feeling down and needing to do something about it. I carried on trying to sleep, but he jerked me wide awake when I heard him say, "It is either a blonde or a bike." There was a pause, in which my heart trip-hammered, but then Hans clarified: "I already have the blonde"—big sigh of relief from me—"so it has to be a bike."

Hans soon regained his total enthusiasm for life by buying a BMW motorbike, and then several more. Vintage models are his great joy, and collecting them and riding them has propelled him into an entirely new chapter, and he now meets biking buddies in all corners of the world. (As I write this, he is keeping out of my way by riding across South Africa.) He also sits on the board of several international BMW clubs and attends global rallies several times a year. I only worry that one day I will be evicted from the bedroom and relocated to the garage so that one of his much-loved bikes can be cuddled up in bed beside him. But he loves it so much!

Guard your enthusiasm carefully. Don't let people who are naysayers for the sake of being naysayers get you down: recognize that it's most likely not your idea that's the issue but their attitude to life. Since you can't totally avoid negative people (some of them will be your nearest and dearest), the only solution is to be prepared for what they might throw at you.

I talked about my dream of restoring an ancient house in Italy for years while I was busy with other things. I knew in my soul it was the right move for me and that one day I would find a way to make it happen.

Still, I talked about it endlessly to friends. One evening, at a big birthday celebration with a group of my pals, I brought it up again at the table. I felt safe surrounded by female friends, most of whom had heard me talk about it before. But one of them clearly had had enough of it, and said, with an actual sneer, "Oh, don't make me laugh, Debbie. You can't even make a bed properly—how can you think of going into the hospitality business? Don't give up your day job!"

I was hurt and humbled, and the next day I found myself mired in destructive second thoughts. She was probably right. Who was I kidding?

My solution and inoculation against this and many other downers? I stuck on my DVD of *Under the Tuscan Sun* and, within minutes, my enthusiasm was restored. I was back in the dream.

One of the best things about a new experience is your childish excitement over what may happen. Never lose the excitement—or let anyone take it away.

COMMANDMENT 10

....

DON'T LOSE YOUR BALANCE

Taking to heart the other nine commandments means nothing if you forget about this one. My own loss of balance was exactly what sparked my next chapter in the first place. Without balance, it is impossible to be comfortable in your skin. We humans work best when we are in tune, inside and out. I cannot stress how important balance is for our health and longevity and the well-being of everyone around us. No one can find or maintain the right balance for you: this is something you have to achieve on your own.

And it's hard, because we're all so busy.

Sorry, can't make the party—it's mental at the office.

Let's get together another time instead.

Can't talk now, I don't even have a second.

We hear these excuses, and we say these things, constantly. Some of us sound proud of our stress levels. I know when someone asks what I've been up to, I feel slightly ashamed if I say, "Well, I had a peaceful walk through the park and hunkered down for the afternoon and read a book." What am I doing, lazing about! We feel we're supposed to be constantly productive and, as a result, most of us are incredibly over-committed. If we aren't, whatever will we post on Instagram or Facebook?

On my own social media, I recently posted a picture of myself trying on a rather sexy dress; it was meant to illustrate a simple comment about Monday blues and cheering yourself up with a bit of shopping. In the photo I looked tanned and slim and pretty great (if I do say so myself). But the picture was seven years old: the dress was the one I ended up wearing as one of the hosts on *Entertainment Tonight*'s coverage of Kate and Will's royal wedding in 2011. As the comments rolled in asking what diet I was on, telling me I looked ten years younger (almost true), I felt like a complete fraud.

It's easy to fall out of true with your own being when your various feeds are bombarding you not only with lots of other people's reactions to your path through life, but also toxic levels of news. I read a column recently by Farhad Manjoo, the "State of the Art" columnist in the Business Day section of the *New York Times*, who decided to try a two-month stint obtaining all his news the old-fashioned way, through print newspapers. Not only did he feel calmer because he got his news fix only once a day, but he also realized that he was feeling better because he was missing the rumours-and-lies phase of each social media news storm, since daily print reporters take care to sift through and verify events. It totally reduced his stress.

Still, life will always get in the way of balance, and it's impossible to feel balanced and happy all the time. I am sure there is a Buddhist monk somewhere having a hissy fit because his robe has shrunk in the wash! The way I think of it is this: when you're in balance, neither your mind, your emotions nor your body is dominating your life. Imagine walking a tightrope. You're moving smoothly, step by steady step, but then the wind blows or your concentration shifts, and you wobble, your arms flail and you lose your balance. To prevent yourself from falling, you have to tap your inner strength, that central core. Then, after that near miss, you need to take a moment to steady yourself and regroup before you can walk forward.

Internal and external elements buffet us as we move through life. Our feelings and state of mind beat at us from the inside. Work, play and relationships batter away from the outside. If we let the externals dictate our path, we sometimes forget to take care of ourselves; I don't know why this is, but it's always somehow easier to just do the thing someone else asks us to do rather than take a moment to reflect on whether that's the right next thing for us to do.

If we get stuck inside our own minds, mired in thoughts and feelings, we miss out on experiencing life itself. Different things may throw us off kilter as we walk our particular tightropes, and all of us need to find our own solid core.

I've found my balance in the simple life. The first time I visited Tuscany I felt stupidly happy. I mean total, heart-swelling joy. Day-to-day life in a Tuscan village was my sweet spot. I didn't worry about fitting exercise into my crazy schedule: walking was a regular part of my day. Eating healthily was easy because it was how everyone around me ate. I got fitter without any stress. This ease

A NEXT ACT THAT JUST FELT RIGHT

TAMARA SIMONEAU

As a television producer for one of the world's most popular entertainment franchises, Tamara had a dream job—travelling to exotic places, mingling with VIPs and chatting with celebrities on the red carpet. Though she grew up in Australia, her home base was Toronto, where she lived with her husband and toddler. Why would you give this up? Every now and then, Tamara still wonders herself, and she told me, "Sometimes there are still moments of panic over what lies ahead."

But she had deep reasons to make a change. Though her life was good, her happiness was undermined by the desperate desire to grow her family in the face of multiple miscarriages and costly fertility treatments. She said, "I'd wait in line at a downtown fertility clinic in the dark hours before the city woke since I had to get to work. I was poked and prodded relentlessly in an exhausting and emotional search for answers. During this miserable time, I made a promise to myself that if another little miracle did come our way, we'd move back to my native Australia, to the laid-back beach life I'd loved as a teenager. I fantasized about the kids diving through the waves after school, eating outside all year long and spending endless hours on the beach, just like I'd done as a child."

When little Ellie at last came along, Tamara did not forget her promise to herself. She packed in her job and the family moved to her homeland. A third baby followed, easily this time. Now Tamara has the children she's always craved and is able to give them the life she lived as a child. "I have an expanse of beach that's almost at our doorstep," she told me. "I watch my kids run free and breathe in the salty air and it is all that I wished for."

Tamara also knows that this blissful new stage in their lives cannot go on forever because it is financially challenging, despite her taking on freelance work for magazines. But she has no regrets: "I have learned that time is the most precious thing we have, and health and youth are right behind. I do miss my old life, but this new chapter is about us, the family, not just me."

of living, this delight in an ordinary moment, propelled me in the direction of my new chapter, which is to share this experience with others.

There is nothing quite so marvellous as the typical Tuscan table. I am always mesmerized when I watch eighteen strangers on the retreat—many of them seeking the balance I found here—laughing and chatting over glasses of wine and an abundance of locally grown food. They are in the moment and enjoying everything that life has to offer. Happiness reigns. After a week of communal meals, of hiking together, of talking together, the biggest question my guests have is "How do I take this feeling home with me and hold on to it?"

You don't need to travel to Tuscany to find balance. You probably don't need a total transformation of your life, either. You can stay at home and set bite-sized goals. Try to eat healthier food and add more exercise to your daily routine: just a short walk will do at first. Make time to see a friend, colleague or family member, not just when there's an obligatory occasion, but to chat. Remember why you love the people you love: they make you happy. Stay away from those who put you in a negative frame of mind and spend more time with the people who make you laugh and feel positive about the future. If your job makes you miserable, you'll never be in balance and eventually your health will suffer. Rethink your job. That may stress you out at first, but if you find a way to earn a living that engages you, you'll be running along that tightrope in no time.

The Commandment Check-up

You have found your dream and you have my commandments at your fingertips, ready to reread when niggling doubts creep near (which they will). Let's affirm each commandment:

1. I have pushed the fear aside. Yes, maybe I'm nervous— even anxious—but I won't let fear hold me back.

2. I have ditched the excuses. I will keep ditching them.

3. I have stopped looking backwards, and regretting all the roads not taken in my life. I am unstuck and ready to move on.

4. I will think about risk in a new way, and I promise to push out of my comfort zone and do things that scare me.

5. I have changed my mindset in order to change the way I look at the world.

6. I know I will make mistakes but I will embrace them, learn from them and move on.

7. I intend to have a good laugh along the way. I am looking forward to laughing more.

8. I will make face-to-face connections and grow through every new alliance.

9. I am excited about this next chapter, thrilled that I can make it happen.

10. Just preparing myself for this new adventure is already making me feel more balanced, but I will look after my health and find ways that help me feel stronger in mind, body and soul.

TIME TO DESIGN YOUR NEXT CHAPTER

Google "happiness" and thousands of quotes float onto your screen. Why? Because we are all searching for it. It can be fun to muse on those quotes; some of them will even shake you up for a moment or two. But even the most inspirational of quotes is not going to lead you to a happier, more fulfilled life. Neither is getting that raise at work, or losing ten pounds, or filling a wrinkle or three with a wee bit of Botox so you look a little younger in the mirror.

No, these are all temporary measures. We need to go deeper. The path to happiness is to discover the joy in something you love to do, something that touches the hidden potential inside you that may have faded, over the years, like a sun-bleached garden cushion. And, actually, the opposite of being depressed is not being happy, it's feeling vital. Vitality is what fades as life throws its spanners into our works. And vitality is what we crave. Being happy all the time is unrealistic, but we can strive to bring vitality back into our lives. That is what will restore the twinkle in our eyes. I guarantee that new adventures outside your comfort zone will reignite your joy in living.

The temptation we all face, though, is to carry on only dreaming, our heads up high in the clouds; it can be really hard to see the steps you need to take to pull off your dream. Remember how many years I just talked about Italy, and watched my trusty DVD of *Under the Tuscan Sun*. But eventually I had to stop drifting inside the romance and jump into the practical planning of how to realize my next chapter.

I asked you to create lists and write yourself letters in the "Dream It" part of this book: get ready for even more homework!

I also want to stress that there is no right or wrong way to transition into a next chapter. But there comes a point where we need to stop the wishful thinking and act. It doesn't matter whether you take a small step or a huge leap: just start moving forward.

In my career as a decorator and designer, I have tackled hundreds of homes, including several of my own. In each one I started with inspiration. Then I broke the project down into chunks, a logical order that every professional or amateur decorator, designer and builder understands, to help me get it done. You can apply the same logic to your new "life" venture, whether you're redesigning what you currently have or starting from scratch. Are you just refreshing the living room with some spring colours, or ripping out the entire kitchen? Are you looking for something that will make your otherwise content life a little more fulfilling, or creating a vision for a brand-new future?

In order to update your life, whether a little or a lot, you need a plan of attack, just as I do when I take on any home renovation. Overalls on, shoulders back—let's get started.

How much change do you need? Just how bad is it? Are you mostly happy with your life, but need a few little improvements, a little more challenge—a simple life tweak? Is your whole life outdated and your days mundane, so you will attempt a larger makeover? Or has the rot infested your entire structure, and you have to tear the whole thing down and rebuild from the ground up? The first step in undertaking this new project is assessing the state you are in.

STEP

1

ASSESS THE SITUATION

Whether you're picking out a new sofa, demolishing and rebuilding a bathroom or renovating the whole nine yards that is your life, don't try to make this assessment all by yourself. Few designers work solo because it is usually much more creative and productive to share ideas and experience with trusted others. When you're assessing a situation, you need to do a great deal of considering, standing around looking at things, hemming

REMEMBER WHAT YOU LIVE FOR

PHILIP RAMBOW

Philip Rambow once announced to everyone sitting around the dinner table with us that I had saved his life. Hardly, but I did help.

I had been asked to be an ambassador for a charitable organization raising funds for research into treatments for prostate cancer. When I met with the staff to discuss what such a role would entail, they mentioned they were holding medical trials of a new treatment protocol in London, England, where Philip was living. I plucked up my courage and asked if a friend of mine would be eligible for the trial. Philip, recently diagnosed with the disease, had decided that he would heal himself through good nutrition. I was worried about him, and was thrilled when the organization agreed to see him. (And bless them, they did not rethink their offer when I couldn't accept the role of ambassador because of conflicts with my TV schedule.)

Philip, slightly reluctantly, went along to meet the researchers. After they checked him out, however, they told him that he was not right for the trial. Worse, they had even more devastating news for him. On the basis of the tests they had run, they told him that unless he had his prostate removed immediately he would probably not live much longer. This woke my dear friend

Philip up; in his secret heart, he had still been thinking that he could self-heal through a healthy diet.

He had the operation. Throughout his recovery, he promised himself that if his cancer was cured, he would live life to the fullest. Born in Montreal, Philip had been a musician and songwriter in his youth, and moved to the UK in the early 1970s to pursue his dream. He'd formed a pub rock band called the Winkies that had gone on tour, opening for Brian Eno; he'd written songs with Kirsty MacColl, and hits for Nick Gilder and Ellen Foley. But even though he'd had such successes, at a point along the way he'd given up on making it in music, and got a day job instead. No more.

When he recovered, Philip returned to songwriting, singing and playing. He found some of his old band members, now retired, and he hired new recruits. Fuelled by his renewed and intense enthusiasm for life, they started performing again. Their new album has just been released, and all the profits are going to prostate cancer research. Philip has never felt happier, or been healthier.

and hawing. I always work with someone who I can bounce ideas off while I think out loud. It makes the entire process bearable and sometimes even fun.

Often you already know the answer. Yes, definitely an antique chandelier goes here. But seeking a second opinion will raise your confidence. Yup, love it, that is the right decision. Sharing your dilemmas with like-minded friends will help you break through roadblocks. This is the time to decide what in your situation is working, what needs to be fixed and what needs to be completely thrown out.

My friend Christine was a popular TV anchor who came into people's homes every evening at 6 p.m. to bring us the news of the day. She'd been hugely successful and was well-loved but when she reached a certain age, her network decided it was time for her to retire. She knew, pretty quickly, that doing nothing was not for her, but she was at a loss as to what came next. If she couldn't be on TV, what else was she fit for? The first year of her "way-too-early retirement" became a painful period of self-assessment that at last led her to an important realization: her skills were in broadcasting, and she was still passionate about it. She had no need to go in search of a new dream, because broadcasting was the job she still wanted to do. It took one chat with a trusted friend over a single glass of wine to formulate a plan. She headed for radio, where ageism went out the window and her talent prevailed. Christine is now happily doing what she knows and loves best, chatting away and entertaining us all. The period she lived through while she was figuring this out wasn't pleasant, but taking that time to assess what she needed to keep and what she needed to change—and to hear thoughts from a nonjudgmental friend—was essential to designing her next chapter.

It is never too late, whatever your age, to start again. In order to start again, though, you likely need a massive emotional clear-out, even when there is plenty from your old life you may wish to salvage. Sometimes, I admit, I've looked at my hubby and wondered if I should put him up for sale on eBay. But each time we rub each other the wrong way, I realize there is still a lot of life left in our marriage, so I keep on trucking with him by my side.

STEP
2

DEMOLISH/
CLEAR OUT/
SALVAGE

It was different with my old career. Even though parts of my television world still thrilled me, there were many elements that left me yawning. I am too young to yawn.

Remember all the decorating shows (including some of my own) that taught us how to be ruthless in prepping for a garage sale by organizing all our stuff into three piles labelled with three handmade signs: CHUCK, SELL/DONATE and KEEP. If you are serious about pursuing a new vision, you need to be equally ruthless about the stuff in your life.

Begin by refurbishing your mind. Clear out the cobwebs and rethink how you do things. Start changing the thought patterns and the beliefs that limit you. For instance, I fly a great deal—usually long transatlantic flights between North America and Europe. I always used to try to work on the plane, but now I relish the seven or eight hours of peace and quiet. I sit and am alone with myself, just me. I focus on the meal, a movie, a book. For the length of the flight, there is nowhere else you have to be—nowhere else you can be. You're trapped, but (as long as you don't suffer from fear of flying!) it's a luxury to be able to chat idly with the person in the seat next to you, to tell all the chores and obligations in your life to take a hike. Tell the worries to take a hike, too. For the next few hours there is nothing you can do about them anyway.

Of course, then you land. Watch what happens around you as everyone grabs for their cellphones and the stress appears again on their faces. It's like we immediately forget that for a short time we had managed to slow down and experience the moment.

So how do we achieve this same kind of decluttering without paying the plane fare? We book the time to throw out all the little aggravations. When they build up again, we stop, take a deep breath, and give them the boot. Don't hang on to those bad memories you worry like a sore tooth. Chuck them out like the broken toys and misplaced socks that linger in the bottom of a cupboard.

Salvage what works—never throw a good idea away, or a good relationship. But toss the stuff that has held you back. A room makeover may require the demolition of a wall to make it larger, more open. The same goes for the mind. Destroy negative thoughts and beliefs, and throw out or at least limit your time with

the naysayers. Salvage the friendships and relationships that bring you joy.

You have to dig deep or only the surface of your life
will be altered. You might be able to nail some new steps
onto that rickety staircase, but what about the rot deep
inside the risers? The only solution is to tear the stairs
out and start afresh.

It can be a formidable challenge but if you do it, you'll
end up with a clear head, a sense of freedom and a sense
of purpose—ready to jump into the planning phase.

Embark on the planning stage by jotting
down all the nightmarish questions that
run through your head like a steam train in
the middle of the night. To get you started,
here are a few that had me wearing out the
floorboards after we bought our property in
Tuscany. They are just as applicable to opening your own yoga studio, starting a cooking
class or designing a new product.

STEP

3

**PLOTTING
AND
PLANNING**

How much is this going to cost to set up?

What if there is no market for what I am offering?

What if it fails?

This project is huge! How do I even start?

After you put these worries down on paper, set
them aside for now. With luck, by articulating your
anxieties, you'll have cleared your head enough to tackle
the next step. Planning is just a more practical form of
dreaming.

When I begin a decorating project, I let my mind run free and list all the possibilities that open up in front of me. Of course, reality soon hits me in the face. That breathtaking kitchen you have on a tear-sheet pinned to the fridge is never going to fit in your tiny house or be built on your minuscule budget. But as you face that fact, you don't fall apart—you compromise and strip elements from what has inspired you and adapt them to the space. Even new handles on the old cupboards and a fresh coat of paint can make a big difference. The same goes for a life redesign.

A designer always puts a timeframe on a project, but rarely keeps to it. Every home I have restored has taken longer than I anticipated. When you are reworking your life, take as long as you need. An extra month or even a year will not matter if you are following your passion. This is important: you don't need to follow anyone else's agenda because this is your next chapter.

Still, it's essential to plan the steps of the journey, just as if you were planning the building, electrics and plumbing on a renovation.

Stick up a large calendar next to the vision board you've created and fill each day with to-do's: people you want to reach out to, meetings you need to take and deadlines for each step. (I like deadlines. They help me think, even if I don't always keep to them.) Schedule time for research and make dates with others to brainstorm and test the project.

Decide if each anticipated milestone will take a couple of weeks, a month or three, or even a year. Breaking

My Italian To-do List

I love nothing more than posting notes to myself and everyone else around my house, though no one but me seems to find it useful. During the final few months of the Italian renovation, when my steady state of anxiety escalated to volcanic eruptions of panic, my lists multiplied like the caged rabbits at the farm up the road. Here, for your amusement, is one from the last two weeks before opening day.

- Get gravel put down on both driveways and all walkways around property
- Get beds into the rooms—chase Roberto for them
- Find out where the duvet covers are
- Unpack all the plates and cutlery
- Tell kitchen supplier that some of the drawers are stuck and need to be unstuck so all the above can be put away
- Ensure all the guests have our phone number in Italy in case they get lost in Rome
- Get an Italian phone number
- Chase up lost luggage (containing fifty logoed water bottles)
- Talk to local farmer about moving his tractor from entrance to our property
- Finish area around pool
- Return the pool towels that turned out to be the size of face cloths. Note to self: measurements are in centimetres not inches
- Find a home for the hedgehogs who are snuggled under the front doorstep
- Tell Alessandro to forget seeding the grass: no time, he should buy sod. Sod it!
- Get aprons for staff
- Get staff
- Go to Florence to pick up stools as company won't deliver
- Tell Hans to finish the wine order
- Don't drink anything until everything is finished
- Put up hammock
- Find a hammock
- Get a manicure and haircut
- Aghhhhh . . .

each phase you need to accomplish into short and long tasks makes them less intimidating.

Keep a journal of your progress. Flipping through it every now and then will give you a bird's-eye view of the project. You'll be able to see which aspects are not developing at the right pace or if you're about to hit a brick wall. Do you want to stop now? Or do you want to get through that wall? If the answer is yes, then you need to plan how you will get over, under or around it.

I've hit that proverbial wall lots of times, and mostly found my way around it. But there is one wall I've never been able to climb over. When I took on the renovation of our villa, people constantly reassured me that I would soon pick up Italian. It was an important skill to have if I was going to direct the builders, negotiate with the suppliers and eventually run a business in Tuscany. But I could never pick up the language. I spent many mornings at a local language school, I hired a private tutor and I downloaded every teaching app that exists. I own DVDs, CDs and many dusty books, but even now I am only capable of throwing a few simple words together in desperate hope that they will make some sense to the Italian who is trying to understand me. When God gave out the brain cells for being a linguist, he forgot me. But when I realized that I was never going to get over the language barrier, my solution was not to give up on my Italian dream but to surround myself with others on this Tuscan hillside who can translate for me. There is only one loser as a result, and that is me. But I figured out how to get by. And I swear that when things settle down a little, I will try again. (Never going to happen.)

RESEARCH

One would never hire a designer or builder without checking them out, canvassing their competition and even visiting some of the places they worked on. You'd never attempt to redecorate a beloved space without making a series of trips to stores, showrooms, home shows and websites, looking for ideas and comparing prices. Pursuing your next chapter depends on doing the research.

Ask yourself:

* What are others doing in this field?

* How long did it take them to get up and running?

* How well are they doing?

* Is there a healthy market for your idea?

Fill notebooks daily with everything you learn in answer to these questions. Let the research guide you; concrete information can help you fend off your anxieties and also deal with the people who want to rain on your parade. Sometimes when you announce that you are really serious about your new chapter—so serious you're starting the necessary research—the people around you may freak out about the risks they assume you're taking.

I recently read a fascinating story in one of the British papers about some women who'd invented a bold new adventure for themselves at a time when they were supposed to be quietly over the hill. I was so intrigued by the story, I managed to track them down and chat with them. Four friends had gone out for dinner: two of them were divorced, two were widowed and all had grown children. Eventually the dinner conversation landed on a painful subject: the necessity, now the kids had gone, of selling their family homes. Their houses were now too big for their needs and too expensive to manage; they each knew they had to downsize to a smaller house or a flat—they didn't really have a choice.

Then their moaning and groaning took a startling turn. What if they each sold up, pooled a portion of their money and together bought a large property they would share, leaving plenty of the proceeds of the sale to live on. I'm of the age where I've had this kind of conversation with women friends (especially the ones living in very expensive cities), but these women decided to act on the idea.

The first roadblock they ran into was the negative reaction of their adult children, who threw every possible problem with such a living arrangement at their mothers. Tantrums are not just for toddlers and teens. The women were disheartened, but they didn't give up. Instead, they began to research.

They met with others who had embarked on a similar idea. They hired accountants and lawyers to work on sorting out the legalities. One of the friends became scared along the way and pulled out, but the remaining three women sold up and together they bought a giant Victorian property on a stunning part of the English coast. They are now living together like students, except they can afford the luxuries that come with this stage in their lives. They grow their own vegetables, cook together and throw plenty of parties, but pay for a cleaning service, repairs and all the aspects of communal living that students can't manage. Their house is full of life and they are never lonely; they each have their own room and the place is large enough that they can enjoy privacy when they need it. There is a constant stream of visitors—including their children, who all came around to the idea in the end, scores of grandchildren and their many friends.

If they'd listened to the doubts expressed by their loved ones, they never would have acted on their idea. Research made them bold.

During the restoration of my dilapidated Tuscan property, I spent years investigating everything from the type of stone to use on the outbuildings to the lighting that would illuminate my new world. I wanted the place to be authentic on the outside but I also wanted all the internal living spaces to be made with highly sophisticated new materials. When it came to the furnishings,

I searched for the best I could afford that would both stay on trend and look awesome for years to come.

While I tackled my building research, I also investigated the world of retreats. What else was out there? What did they charge? What type of clients did they attract?

All in the name of research (of course!), I visited yoga retreats in India (cheap, rustic and fun with a bunch of friends); fancy wellness centres in Arizona (expensive and often a hard place to meet others); a cooking retreat in Italy (lively, but it didn't leave me with much to take home besides recipes); and a boot camp in France that resulted in aches in muscles I didn't know I had and left me depressed that I would never be able to maintain the regimen I'd learned when I limped back to real life.

I visualized the women who would attend my retreats coming for their own unique week, each moment of which would be like a "girls' night out." I wished to give them an experience they would never forget, that would allow them to feel special. This was the type of retreat I craved for myself! The best advice I can give anyone starting a passionate new project is to not only follow your gut but build on what you yourself would want. This focus will rarely let you down.

I could feel this Tuscan adventure in my bones. I envisioned the guests as they arrived, imagined their first sight of the breathtaking view, felt their emotions as each of them took in the suite and private garden that would be hers to enjoy for a whole week. I dreamed of inspiring them with our simple lifestyle on this ancient land and of offering them a variety of tools to enable them to follow their own vision.

When I designed the semi-professional kitchen, I insisted on a five-metre-long stone island. I had a mental picture of eighteen women sipping Prosecco around it as they took part in a boisterous cooking class, giggling like schoolchildren as they rolled out ribbons of fresh pasta. Of course, when the island arrived it was way too long—the black volcanic stone resembled an airport runway. It had to be removed and shortened at great expense. (Yes, this decorator makes many mistakes.) But my eighteen weekly guests still fit around that slab, and the cooking classes are just as entertaining as I thought they would be. The laughter and silliness shakes the chestnut-wood rafters as grown women, who have been cooking all their lives, turn into giggling thirteen-year-olds at a birthday party.

I could also imagine the nightly forums we would hold under a giant olive tree or snuggled together around the firepit. Here these women would share stories, glasses brimming with local wine. The picture in my head told me I would need a bar beside the forum site, so I built one from an enormous fallen tree trunk. This space is now exactly as I envisioned it, and is the most popular area on the property.

CLARIFYING BODY AND SOUL

SUSANA BELEN

I met Susana Belen twelve years ago at We Care Spa, the highly rated fasting and detoxing spa she owns in Palm Springs. I love detoxing for the simple reason that, afterwards, I feel clear-headed and ready to tackle whatever project I am embarking on. The story of how Susana got into the business, which she told me on that first visit, has stayed with me.

She and her family moved to Los Angeles from Argentina. Shortly after they arrived, Susana and her husband broke up, leaving her alone with four children and barely able to speak English. She struggled to cope, but anger, stress and sadness led to depression. A friend suggested Susana meet with a local holistic doctor, who took Susana off her typical South American diet of meat and potatoes and introduced her to a serious detox by way of juice fasting. (This was over thirty years ago, long before juicing became an international phenomenon.) Not only did her depression lift, but Susana found herself moving through her long hard days with renewed energy. She became intrigued by the health benefits of cleansing.

Susana read everything on the subject she could get her hands on. She travelled to clinics in Mexico and the Far East to study their practices. The more she learned, the more she shared her knowledge with others who also needed this kind of change in their lives.

Eventually she bought some cheap land in the desert and opened a tiny spa; it was so modest she put some of the clients up in trailers. These days, people come from all over the world to her now stunningly designed spa, including a constant stream of celebrities and other stressed-out, exhausted people who wish to detox their bodies and their souls. It was finding herself at such an unhealthy crossroads and following a path of renewal that gave Susana, now in her late seventies, her own next chapter.

Jump into the research with relish. Your new chapter is your baby, and you need to learn everything you can about it. Research will show you which ideas you need to abandon, yes, but it will also spark the imagination and inspire you to explore new angles. It will open you to more opportunities and will lead you to new people who can help. Most of us who have walked a similar path appreciate sharing our stories, both the successes and the failures. The more you get out there and discover, the more of what you learn will become your own.

STEP

5

**IMPROVE
YOUR
DIGITAL
MARKETING
KNOW-HOW**

My children will scream with laughter when they find out I'm giving out social media advice. They are right about how unlikely this is, of course. I struggle to understand what is so very easy for my sons' generation.

But I have come to appreciate its value. When I launched each of my five television series, the networks spent fortunes on promotion. I was what is known in the business as "promotable"—which means I could bring in viewers. The network's job was to make sure that all the fans were aware of any new show I was in. As a result, I appeared on massive billboards on the sides of buildings, on posters in bus stops, in commercials playing on the radio and television: the advertising budgets must have been insane. The same went for my product lines at one of the world's largest retailers. Again, I appeared in nonstop print and television commercials. It was wonderful. But reality sets in when you need to promote a new project with no backing from big networks or corporations. This is when social media outreach is your best friend. The biggest investment you'll make at first is your time, which you need to spend learning how to reach the widest audience. It also has to be the right audience—people who are interested in what you in particular have to offer. Then you have to deliver information and images about your product and your journey that will intrigue them. I find that the weirdest thing is that, unlike old-fashioned print and broadcast advertising, not much of social media communication is about directly selling anything. To fill the spots at our Tuscan retreats we relied on a little press, on social media postings and on word of mouth. All worked successfully, and the result is that we're often fully booked. I have no idea how small businesses ever managed before the internet.

My best advice on taking your first steps in this mind-boggling new world is to ask for help from anyone you know who is under twenty-five and not one of your own kids. (I find that pinning one of my sons' friends down for advice produces better results and I have to survive less impatience; also, the friends think it's impolite to say no!) A crucial decision is picking which platform works best for you and the age group you wish to attract.

BAKING UP A BIG SUCCESS

ALEXANDRA HARDING

A stay-at-home mom with two small children, Alex was always happiest in the kitchen, especially when she was baking. When both of her kids were diagnosed with severe food allergies, one to nuts and the other to eggs, she had to get creative. She says, "I felt so sad for them when they returned from yet another party and could not tuck into the desserts with the other kids. I began by making extra-special cupcakes and treats for them." It turned out she was excellent at finding ways to handle food allergies and sensitivities and still create delicious baked goods from the very best ingredients. The word got around and soon the requests were pouring in for her to make the celebratory sweet treats for parties and weddings, and she decided to morph her hobby into a business. She had her own doubts about whether her hobby would still be fun when she had to get up at the crack of dawn and work to the wee small hours of the morning to meet the demand, and she faced her share of doubters with glass-half-empty worries over how she would handle the financials alongside all the baking and who would watch the kids? But so far it's all worked out: Alex has been running Vintage Rose Cupcakes—literally a cottage industry—in the picturesque town of Tunbridge

Wells in Kent, England, for the last seven years. Who better to answer the kind of questions anyone thinking of transforming a hobby into a business may ask?

WHAT WAS YOUR INSPIRATION?

I live in an area where there are many mompreneurs working on everything from curtain making to creating a variety of gifts. They worked from home, enabling them to still be there for their kids. If they could do it, I was confident I could give it a shot.

HOW DID YOU ADVERTISE YOUR TALENTS?

At first, completely word of mouth. Then Facebook, Pinterest, Instagram and Twitter. For my type of business visuals are imperative. My husband helped me set up a website and that is the foundation of getting the orders. It is mostly an online business.

HOW COULD YOU AFFORD TO TAKE ALL THE STUNNING PICTURES YOU HAVE ON YOUR WEBSITE AND SOCIAL MEDIA FEEDS?

I joined up with a group of local people who were making wedding apparel, florists and caterers and we shared the cost of professional photography and then sent the images off to blogs and magazines. This approach not only gets our products noticed, but it can get lonely in my kitchen, so I really look forward to these times when I can work alongside other entrepreneurs and share ideas and problems.

HOW MUCH DID YOU INVEST IN THE BAKING BUSINESS WHEN YOU BEGAN?

Nothing, except for flour, eggs and sugar, really. It was a big day when I made enough profit to buy my first professional mixer.

HAVE YOU THOUGHT OF MOVING OUT OF YOUR HOUSE INTO A COMMERCIAL KITCHEN?

I think about moving into a commercial kitchen all the time. I have already worn out my first oven. I am onto the second one now.

WHAT IS STOPPING YOU?

It is a big leap and it comes with a mass of financial commitments, travel and time away from the kids. It is important for me to grow the business organically. I feel that for now the priority should be getting the wedding cakes out on time and keeping the clients happy.

WHAT ARE SOME OF THE NEGATIVES?

Well, I have to wear many hats. I design, bake and shop. I am the accountant and my own customer service rep.

I am the brand ambassador and the CEO of my company and the constant washer-upper. Though, when it gets super busy, I do get some help. Some days it's just work, not fun, but most of the time I really adore what I do.

IS THERE A NEXT NEW CHAPTER TO YOUR NEW CHAPTER?

I have lots of plans: when you are alone in the kitchen it gives you plenty of time to think. In another few years, the children will be leaving home. I will be an empty nester and this will be the time to expand, maybe open my own shop. For now, everyone is happy and I am excited about future dreams.

Instagram works really well for my retreats. Also, people following you on Instagram don't expect you to post multiple times a day—every couple of days will do. On Twitter, occasional posting won't get you a following. Twitter users expect you to tweet several times a day, as Twitter rests on the idea that you're tweeting thoughts as they occur to you in relation to the day's events. You won't realize these things, though, unless you investigate them with the help of a good guide!

I know it is overwhelming. It seems like there is something new to learn every day. One minute Facebook is the communication vehicle of choice, and the next it's Instagram and Pinterest. Who knows what it'll be by the time you hold this book in your hands. Stay nimble, as the business gurus say, and don't fight the times we live in. There is really no point.

Though sometimes going old school can still be effective. Several years ago, I was giving a speech at a university, feeling intimidated by all the shining young faces looking back at me. I was talking about the importance to their potential careers of building contacts and I hit one of my perennial points, about how eye-to-eye, face-to-face contact is still important in the age of social media. When I mentioned how much I still valued my Rolodex, I knew what would come next. Sure enough, several hands shot up, because very few of the crowd knew what a Rolodex was.

I explained, to their amusement, that it was a way to organize and store business cards and contacts alphabetically, so they were at your fingertips. I knew they all stored that kind of information in their phones, but I described how advantageous a physical business card could be—good to the touch, beautifully designed, an embodiment of how you want to display yourself to the world. (And with so many printing services offering templates you can customize, they are cheap to design and make.) But also, I explained, whenever someone offered me a card I always made a note on it of a crucial detail of our meeting. Then I added the new card to one of my Rolodex's organizational categories: referrals, business competitors, leads, manufacturers, and so on. That way I didn't end up with a big mass of cards in a pile and no idea who any of them were.

To my surprise, the students embraced the idea of collecting business cards within a Rolodex as if I'd invented something worthy of a Nobel prize. Sometimes an idea that is completely obvious to you is a revelation to someone else.

Last note: if social media and the world of technology are just too painful for you to take on yourself, this is where it's worth it to hire someone. You need this stuff to succeed in today's world. Which I know you know, but just as with the business cards and the students, it's worth reinforcing.

STEP

6

**PRACTISE,
PRACTISE,
PRACTISE**

I cannot stress how important the "practice makes perfect" adage is to launching a next chapter. Even in relationships, if you're thinking of hooking up with someone permanently, travel with them first. Travel brings out the best and the worst in us, but mostly the worst. I used to tell my sons, "If you still like her after a long road trip, several nights in a cheap motel and a massive fight during a highway breakdown in a snowstorm, then you're probably safe to move in together . . ."

When I blurted out onstage the idea of holding getaways in Tuscany, I knew the first step was to try one. My heart told me I also needed my best friend by my side. I've known Jacky Brown for over thirty years, and I know her better than anyone outside my immediate family. I was nineteen when I first saw her, after she walked into a sushi bar in downtown Tokyo. She was elegant and beautiful, as always. I was at a table surrounded by a group of models who were all helplessly laughing as I held court. The plastic bottle I'd been holding had just exploded and my white linen suit was covered in ketchup. I thought it was hysterical, too. Jacky also found it funny that the accident had happened because I was covering my sushi rolls in ketchup. One of the reasons we've managed to remain best friends, apart from our crazy adventures together, is that our four sons and our husbands also like each other: we are lucky.

Jacky was on board with the Tuscan idea immediately and we leapt into our test run. I flew to the area of Italy where Hans and I had been searching for a property (by that point we knew it well) and found an old villa to rent that would accommodate all the guests and ourselves. Hidden under all the cobwebs was a beautiful building, but it was a mess. Piles of mismatched furniture sat on grimy stone floors. Clouds of dust swirled around my ankles as I walked across the threadbare rugs. Half the light bulbs were missing, leaving a dull pall over the interior. But the bones were good, the linens acceptable, the plumbing worked and the surrounding landscape was truly Tuscan.

We set to work. Rugs were rolled up and hidden away, and the furniture thinned out; a few brightly coloured throws hid the ugly sofas. It's surprising how bunches of wild flowers can transform the most desperate room. I borrowed metal chairs from a local restaurant to replace the white plastic ones and the guys knocked together some rustic benches and tables for the garden. Within days, the place looked warm and inviting. When the vans rolled down the long, hedged driveway and chattering women tumbled out onto the stone forecourt, the evening sun drenched the plastered walls in gold and the world smiled.

We practised every aspect of running a retreat during that first week. Everything that could go wrong went wrong. (It really does not matter what kind of business you run, there will always be drama. The trick is to be ready to act, be decisive and stay calm.) We had to deal with two sets of lost luggage and one lost person who had roamed away across a neigbouring field. The luggage never arrived but we found our wanderer several miles away, oblivious to the search party. One distraught woman was stung by a bee and suffered a nasty allergic reaction. It turned out she had not brought her EpiPen with her because she did not think there were bees in Italy!

One day the chef fell ill and never turned up, and neither did the food. But after one of the guests found me sobbing into a nearly empty fridge, the meal turned into a magical evening. She rallied the entire group, who prepared a stupendous dinner from leftovers.

We had an invasion of angry wasps that dive-bombed the swimming pool, forcing everyone to take shelter inside the villa. After a few frantic phone calls, six burly Italian firemen arrived to demolish the nest. To the delight of all the women, after the firemen had done their job on the wasps, they joined them for a swim and well-deserved cold beers.

After the first retreat, which all the guests deemed a memorable success, we made sure we were equipped with plenty of remedies, antidotes, defences and numerous Band-Aids. After the second retreat we also knew what would never work, and that was the layout of the building. As the village bells struck midnight—and everyone, we presumed, was tucked up for the night—two guests caught Hans sneaking a beef sandwich in the kitchen wearing only his boxers. He was by far more embarrassed than the two women were, but we realized that having both the guests and ourselves under one roof was not ideal. We needed our privacy and so did they.

The home we now live in is perfect for that exact reason. The original rundown villa was surrounded by pigsties that could be transformed into suites, without the piggies, of course. Each guest now enjoys her own entrance, her own little space and a private garden, while we live in the villa. Now there is little likelihood that some midnight wanderer will bump into a partially dressed Hans, shocking them both!

You are likely hoping it won't be a million-dollar question, but it's a big one: How do you fund your dream?

I confess that my least favourite words all have to do with money. Financing, capital, borrowing, savings, income, expenses, bills, profit, loss: they all come under the budget heading. Much as I shrink from the idea, I am afraid that a budget for your next chapter is one of the most important priorities that needs to be addressed. Just as with designing a home, designing your new chapter requires a good deal of money management.

Pursuing a new dream, a new life, a new project, does not have to cost you much. In fact, at first it may cost nothing except your time—your "sweat equity." But even if the venture itself doesn't cost that much, you still have to live while you're launching it. Before

STEP

7

BUDGET

you turn your dream into reality, it is imperative
that you put aside enough funds to keep you and your
family secure for the first months or even years. If you're
in a relationship, can your partner support you while
you get going without causing too much hardship or
resentment? You also need to create a back-up plan in
case your dream does not work out. Money helps.

For instance, we did not pay the villa rental for our
first practice retreat in Italy until we'd signed up the
guests and taken their deposits. The only cash investment we made off the top was to pay for our flights
back and forth to Italy and those colourful throws to
hide the horrible couches; instead we invested our
labour with buckets and brooms, hauling furniture,
begging and borrowing. Only after the first retreats
were a success did we take the plunge and invest in the
project long term. So think hard about what you really
need to get going.

Here are the primary money questions you need to
answer.

1. **How much is it going to cost to start my new chapter?**
    You've done the research and established what
    your idea will involve. Either you tackle trying
    to figure out the budget on your own or you
    seek out professional help to tailor a business
    model (probably a good investment in the long
    run). Whichever path you choose, your business
    model needs to include everything you require
    to get up and running. Do you need to pay rent

on an office or a location space or can you work out of your home? Do you need to purchase supplies and equipment to start the venture? What will you live off while you get going?

2. **Can I afford to quit my present job to follow my dream?**

If you have savings that can tide you over, you may be able to start full time on the new venture right off the bat. But if you don't, you need to hang on to your job as you launch your next chapter. This will mean longer hours and definitely more late nights and weekends as you remain at the full-time job while using all your spare time to pursue the dream job. A woman I know named Nina hung on to her position as an executive assistant and an office manager as she slowly pursued her passion for furniture and interior design. Many a family vacation took her to places where she could scout lines that no one else was selling in her city. Colleagues and friends soon were asking for her advice, and paying her to source things for them. After a build of about five years, where she was able to bridge her full-time job and her aspirations, she was finally able to quit her job with a website and a retail space already up and running: she'd established that there was a clientele for her taste and for the furniture she wanted to import. She was dogged and clever, but also very conscious that she couldn't risk the financial well-being of her family.

Here's another example of taking it slowly. After Fiona graduated from university as a psychologist, she had a tough time finding the right career in her field. So while she pursued every avenue, she also trained as a yoga teacher to support herself. It took her several patient years of teaching downward dog and sun salutations before she was able to join the Red Cross in Central Africa. Yoga was her route to happiness as a humanitarian.

Gillian could not wait. She decided she had to quit her corporate job outright in order to pursue her dream to become a teacher. Even though she didn't have the money to go to teachers college, she did not give up. Instead, Gillian joined an agency that hired teachers of English as a second language for jobs in a variety of countries. Money now was no barrier: her flights were paid for and her accommodation was organized. Soon she was not only fulfilling her wish to teach, she was also seeing the world. She has already worked with children in South Korea and Morocco, and is presently in Argentina.

3. **What if I do not have the funds to start something new?** There are plenty of exciting dreams to pursue that do not require much money. Maybe you could think about what you could do with

a hobby you love. As I've mentioned, my own career in front of the camera grew out of my "hobby" of painting; the difference between a hobby and a next chapter really comes down to whether you dream of working at it full time and whether you can support yourself while you do it. At first, I painted my own walls, and then I painted walls for my relatives, and then one day someone actually paid me to tackle their house, and I was away!

Remember Sian, my sister-in-law, who so bravely shared the fears she faced as both her daughters were on their way to college? Sian had worked in public relations before deciding to stay home with her girls, and she wasn't sure about going back to the same kind of job. But the question loomed: How would she fill her days and support herself after the girls left home? She began to take long walks around Manhattan every morning after her youngest daughter had left for school. She needed to think, and walking for hours both eased her anxiety and helped clear her head. As she hoofed it around the Big Apple, she began to see this great city with fresh eyes. Soon she was taking photos of things that struck her as she pounded the sidewalks. A friend suggested she set up an Instagram account and post her pictures. She did, and the "likes" grew rapidly. Within a few months every single major American television network had

HER MOTHER'S DAUGHTER

KAREEN HAGUE

Many of us aren't able to take the risk of leaving our current jobs in order to follow a dream. But that doesn't mean you can't transform your life. Kareen, who came to one of our retreats in 2016, told us that she had worked for a knitwear company in Toronto for more than twenty years. Though she experienced the usual ups and downs of any job, she was fairly happy until her mother was diagnosed with dementia.

Her mother was a successful artist and Kareen had grown up around her paintings, and always gone to her exhibitions and openings. When her final days arrived, the family surrounded her with the artwork she had made over her life. It was horrible to lose such a creative woman, but grief inspired Kareen to take up her mother's brushes and start painting. Soon she was taking part in exhibitions and selling her own pieces.

Her life is now extremely full. "When I am not at work," she said, "I am painting." She is not quite ready to let go of the financial security of her full-time job for the uncertainty of an artist's life. "What is exciting, though, is that I am ready. The day will come when I feel it is the right time to jump completely into this new stage in my life and my art will become my profession."

either reposted her photos on their own sites or had used them to illustrate their weather reports. Though they didn't pay her to use the shots they always gave her a credit. She found it thrilling at first, but eventually she started to wonder about whether her hobby could pay.

Then an Instagram follower asked if she could buy a print. More and more requests came in. Sian was ecstatic, and started exploring the possibilities with different printers. Pretty soon she was selling her work, and that has turned into a small but growing business. The thought of life after her youngest daughter heads to college now doesn't seem so scary.

What thrills me about Sian's story is that when I started writing this book, she was unhappy about her circumstances and in preemptive mourning over her loss of identity as a mother. As I finish the book, she is launched on a whole new chapter that flows out of her great eye and passion for the world around her, and a talent she's just discovered.

4. **I need funds to get started but I have no collateral or assets. Would a bank even loan me the money?**

Probably not, but you can beg, borrow or steal. Well, not steal, but beg and borrow for sure. Or not even "beg" . . . how about trade?

Offer your services to friends, colleagues and family in return for supplies. I painted a printer's living room, who in payment printed the video sleeves for my how-to-paint demonstrations. I produced and sold those VHSs (remember those?) in several languages, and they caught the eye of several paint brands in North America. I then recorded versions for each manufacturer that promoted their particular paint. I used the proceeds of this financial triumph to produce my first television series, which was all about paint. By bartering a beautifully painted living room for services from my friendly printer, I was able to move up to the next level of the entrepreneurial ladder.

A friend of mine had chosen the path of being a stay-at-home mom but on finding herself divorced and an empty nester, she had to earn a living. She had always been an accomplished seamstress and for years had helped many friends and neighbours by running up curtains for their homes. So she decided to launch a career making bespoke drapes and blinds, but she needed funds to get started. It was payback time for all the help she'd given others over the years. She not only contacted everyone she'd helped, but everyone she knew, and invited them all to a weekend barbecue. The food was great and she waited until everyone had eaten and was having a wonderful time. Then she told them all that she had an announcement to make. She shared her dream plan, and then she asked her guests to please donate what they could to help her rent a small studio and buy a sewing machine. No one thought this was cheeky or pushy. In fact, they were so enthusiastic they donated more money than she'd hoped for and also placed orders for her first batches of curtains.

I know this is another old chestnut, but where there is a will there is always a way.

5. **How do I approach the bank for a loan?**

I find it terrifying. Meeting with a lender can make your heart pound, your hands tremble and your knees shake. I don't know why it's so scary; the worst that can happen is they say no!

It is imperative that before you head into a meeting with a potential lender, you do your homework. Begin by asking for help from anyone you think might have sound advice. Which banks are the best to approach for your kind of venture? What questions should you ask and what information should you bring with you? What questions will the lender ask? Is anyone you know able to give you a personal introduction to the lender? Knowledge will help ease the nerves.

You will require a business plan that is clear not only to yourself but to the banker. Be prepared, rehearse what you need to say and also ask the banker questions about their process so you're sure you understand. And be ready for the prime question the bank will want you to answer: How will you be able to pay the money back?

6. **How do I find an investor?**

I cannot stress enough what a huge step it is to take on a partner, whether solely on the financial side or to share the work. Some partnerships are things of beauty, but a large proportion do not work out. Partnering with a spouse is a whole other kettle of fish—as I can attest after thirty years of working with mine. On the domestic front, Hans has never stacked a dishwasher—that's my job, and I've given up whining about it. I, however, am basically allergic to finances, so Hans has given up on me on that front: that's his job, both in our married life and in our businesses. Our collaboration has not always been pretty, but by applying the right amount of respect and giving each other a wide rein in our particular areas of expertise, we've made a success of it. The great advantage of working with a spouse is that both of you get to share equally in the rewards of your success and you're both committed to the family's well-being. But—and this is a massive but—if it doesn't work out, it can be messy.

If you're searching for an outside partner, get the word out that you are looking for investment. Canvass everyone you know: friends, friends of friends, old colleagues, new colleagues. If you are very brave, and you know the person you are thinking of can afford to lose some money, don't be afraid to ask family. Otherwise, never ask! Angel investors—pros who work for investment banks—are another option. They are usually prepared to take greater risks than your friends and family are, but they will also want a larger stake in your venture. And sometimes local communities offer small business development funds you can tap into, which you can often find through community colleges and regional government offices.

Any investor, small or large, a relative or a professional, will want to know that your venture has a decent chance of success, that you have thought it through, that you have the courage and discipline to persevere, that you've done your research: all these things will reassure them that their money is relatively safe.

Beware of charlatans—the entrepreneurial world is rife with them. Ask as many questions of your potential investor as they are asking of you.

I guess my best advice is to move ahead on the money front at a snail's pace. If you don't have to borrow, then don't borrow! At a certain point in life, the glory of starting a new chapter is that it's not so much about becoming a billionaire as about waking up each morning overflowing with energy about the day ahead.

The Money Checklist
Whether you have begged or borrowed or are investing
your own savings, be prepared to be lean and mean
with yourself for quite a while.

1. **ASSESS YOUR FINANCIAL SITUATION:** What do you have, what do you owe, what do you need?

2. **GET PROFESSIONAL HELP:** Sit down with someone from a financial institution and go through your options.

3. **IF YOU ARE PLANNING EARLY RETIREMENT IN ORDER TO FOLLOW YOUR DREAM,** talk to the company that organizes your retirement plan and see what your options are.

4. **IF YOU ARE GOING BACK TO SCHOOL TO TRAIN FOR A NEXT CHAPTER,** you may have to take on part-time work. With luck, you'll find it in the field you are training in.

5. **IF YOU ARE OLDER AND HAVE DECIDED TO USE YOUR SAVINGS, SET A LIMIT ON WHAT YOU CAN AFFORD TO LOSE.** The older you are the less time you have to earn those savings back.

6. **BE FRUGAL.** Don't spend unless it's absolutely necessary. Taking extra care with your expenditures could be what makes or breaks your venture.

7. **IF YOU ARE PLANNING TO PROVIDE A SERVICE, MAKE SURE YOU KNOW HOW YOU WILL BE PAID.** When I began painting houses for money, I asked for a partial payment up front; I also charged for my consultations with the clients before I took the job on. Decorators and designers often find asking for such a payment incredibly difficult, but in my experience if a client is willing to pay a nominal fee for that consultation, they are more likely to go ahead and book the job. It weeds out the people who just want to talk about it. (I always returned the consultation fee after the job was finished.)

8. **PLAN TO INVOICE PROMPTLY.** In Italy we are still getting bills from some of our tradespeople years after they did the work because they never seem to make the time to do their paperwork. No one wants to pay a bill years after the work was done!

9. **I KNOW THINGS JUST GOT VERY REAL AS YOU READ THIS LIST.** But don't let the fear of financing your new chapter hold you back. If this is something you are meant to do, you will find a way.

LIVE IT

LIVING WITH THE CONSEQUENCES

I had dreamed of living in Tuscany ever since Frances Mayes enthralled me, as a stressed-out mother of two trying to juggle a television career, with *Under the Tuscan Sun*. When I realized that I had to make a concrete, radical change in my life, Italy was the direction I turned in. I did my research and we did our budgeting. We planned it out to the smallest details, and all of it was exciting.

The "do it" part of the adventure was not quite so dreamy.

Hans and I began each day of our five-year renovation by consulting our endless to-do lists. We restored three buildings and two courtyards, transformed a set of pigsties and built a pool (my first), along with digging out a lake I called Lake Como—really more of a wildlife pond. On top of this, we became farmers, though my sweet husband had never planted so much as a window box in his previous life. Still, he threw himself into this unknown pursuit with the same devotion he gives to one of our new television productions.

Along with the villa, as I mentioned, we'd taken on over twelve hundred olive trees that had to be pruned and harvested, and a craggy old vineyard that produced the oddest wine (and I can drink anything). While it tasted good, indulging in several glasses of "Chateau Reniella" resulted in a headache that began at the ankles and steadily rose through every joint in the body until it attacked the brain. So we also had to take on the task of learning to make drinkable wine, alongside olive farming and dealing with the bureaucracy of being classified as an organic farm. Not easy in any country, but the piles of paperwork required in Italy will have your head spinning and your thoughts turning to running back to the city.

The days never went as planned, and the daily chores were rarely completed. Life in Italy has its own pace and in Tuscany that pace gets taken down another notch. Every day I heard, "Debbie, *tranquillo*." Relax. (I still hear it all the time.)

In June 2015, we opened the gates to Villa Reniella after five arduous years of battling the Italian bureaucracy, attempting to learn the language and working daily with a huge crew of builders and tradespeople. The first was a nightmare, the second dismal (as I've confessed) and the last a joy.

When the first group of eighteen ecstatic women arrived, they burst out of the vans onto my sun-drenched white-river-stone driveway under azure skies. The giddy chatter stopped. They clustered beneath statuesque cypress trees and there was a communal intake of breath as they stared out at the view. High on the hill across the valley lay the medieval town of Montepulciano surrounded by vineyards, swaying wheat fields and an abundance of olive groves. Many began to cry. I was crying too. Hans looked bemused and mouthed at me, "What's wrong?"

Nothing was wrong! Everything was right: the women were here—finally here. As we handed each of them a glass of chilled Pinot Grigio, every woman knew that the coming week would be more than they had ever imagined.

I felt the same way. I had envisioned this exact moment for years. The work was done and my dream was fulfilled. Now I was living it.

It took only minutes for someone to burst my bubble: a worried guest realized she had left her passport in the hotel safe in Rome.

So you pulled it off and launched your next chapter. You have opened your own business, found a way to give back in a far-off land, decided to take a pay cut to finally devote yourself to what you love. And likely you've ended up in one of these three situations.

The first: be careful of what you wish for. Reality has set in, the dream has burst, and there's egg on your face.

The second: the dream did not work out as planned but it led you to an alternate path and an unexpected new possibility materialized.

The third: Everything is idyllic. The dream turned out to be all you imagined it to be, and you're living in utopia. (Okay, I'm laughing now, because this third one is impossible.)

Reading this may feel like being dunked in cold water, especially if the book has brought you to the point where you're buzzing with enthusiasm for your own new beginning. I don't want to dampen your eagerness and I need you to stay positive. But I also would feel awful if I painted this next phase as all moonbeams and rosebuds, and ignored the always messy business of being human.

Let's think about the first scenario. The new venture was a disaster. This can happen, and it has happened to me too many times to count. But I never let fear of things not working out hold me back, and you shouldn't either.

Kyle and Joanna went on their dream holiday to a Greek island. Newly married, they spent their days on a local sun-kissed beach and lounged through long lunches under a vine-covered pergola at the rustic beach taverna. Sounds like paradise? In their eyes it was, and it was also life-changing. As they sipped glasses of chilled rosé and tucked into squid kebabs with their bare toes snuggled into the warm sand, they began to fantasize. It turned out that the little beach restaurant was for sale. By the end of the trip, they had made a decision. Since they were young, childless and free of other important commitments, they sold their home back in Texas and with the proceeds bought their dream. Within six months, they were living on the island of Paros.

It is a breathtaking island, as I know, because I too spent my honeymoon there during a long, sunny July. It's stunning in the summer, but not so much in the colder months. That first winter on Paros, the couple moved into a room at the back of their new restaurant and the island experienced its first snow in forty years. Then gales swept in and destroyed the tavern on the beach. They lost everything.

They were sunk before they even started, and they were rightly devastated by their losses. But they also found that they had changed. They couldn't imagine retreating to Texas, back to the daily drudgery of their former office jobs, the tyranny of mortgage payments, and all of their past routines.

Once they'd recovered from the shock, they brushed themselves off and pressed the refresh button on their dream. To make ends meet, Kyle took a job in a nearby restaurant, and for a time so did Joanna (but she was pregnant by then—talk about extra worry!). Here friendships were formed as they worked alongside the locals and other expats, and soon these new friends were helping them to rebuild their home, their business and their future. Kyle told me that later he realized if disaster hadn't struck, he and Joanna would never have formed such secure relationships so soon, and their restaurant would likely have failed.

If you dare to dream, you live with the consequences. Whatever they may be.

A new chapter is exactly that, a new chapter in your life's own book. You reach the end of one, and if you do not turn the page, you will never know what might have happened next. Who goes on a new adventure, yet meets no one and learns nothing along the way? This is not possible. Life itself guarantees some form of drama. Only those with their eyes tight shut and their front doors firmly locked will gain nothing from trying something new. If you fail, you also learn a lot, as Kyle and Joanna did. I guarantee it. Let the failure guide you to the next step.

Maybe you have realized that, next time around, you would do things differently, get yourself a partner, work with a larger group, or follow a different road to your goal. I have listened to many people who have attempted to transition into a role they were passionate about and it didn't work out. But I have not met a single one of them who regretted trying or felt that the effort was a waste of time. All of them believed that they had grown through their experience, and felt they had changed for the better. The more you try to do, the more you want to do and the more you can do. Each time you fall, it gets easier, surprisingly, to get back up. It is as if experience finally teaches us to trust that each disappointment will lead us to another open door.

Most of us have experienced Scenario 2. We chased a dream but, when we caught it, it wasn't anything like we expected it to be.

One of the most vivid examples I've seen of this comes from Marni Wasserman, a young guest at one of my retreats. Women who apply fill in a registration form where they answer several questions, including this one: "What would this week mean to you?" (Some write pages in response.) Marni wrote that she was excited about the opportunity to attend our retreat and that it was special because she would be coming on her honeymoon. That was a first! I double-checked with her to make sure she understood that the retreats were women-only and she assured me that she did. Okay, each to her own, I thought.

She arrived looking nothing like a young woman happily enjoying her honeymoon; after all, she was here with us while her bridegroom had gone cycling. Though she animatedly took part in all the forums, we could tell something was not right with her new marriage. She had previously trained as a nutritionist and chef and was running a cooking school out of her parents' kitchen where she taught others about the benefits of eating well. At the end of the retreat, she told me that the quality of the homegrown food, the vegetable gardens and the simple Tuscan meals she'd enjoyed all week had confirmed her passion for healthy eating—but not for her new spouse.

I am sure there was much more to this story, but a few months after she flew home, Marni separated from her husband and was re-inspired in her career. She was successful in filling her classes but found the challenges and limitations of working out of her parents' home to be too daunting and she decided to open her own brick and mortar food studio in downtown Toronto. That venture was successful, but eventually she began to think beyond a cooking school as the best means to reach people with her message. Drawing on everything she'd learned about food and nutrition and the way people's lives are transformed by healthy eating, she began *The Ultimate Health Podcast* with her partner (and now husband), Jesse Chappus. It has been a roaring success; every week Marni and Jesse interview world-acclaimed writers, doctors and journalists.

In the end, to follow her dream, she let go of her first marriage, and then her cooking school, which opened the doors to a new relationship and a new career in which she could inspire more people.

The time you spend creating a new approach to life will open you up to other opportunities too. So if your plan doesn't work out the way you thought it would, leave your discouragement behind and move on. This is what a vital life is all about—not success or failure, but the constant search for the place we want to be, the place where we are whole and totally engaged.

In the third situation, you end up really living the dream. But you can't predict what the true consequences will be when you move to another country, start that business, shed your old life in favour of meaningful engagement in a charity or in teaching, or any of the other paths the people I've written about in this book have chosen. Even a new relationship is a beginning. My maternal grandmother was beautiful, glamorous and a little wild, and she married several times. I remember meeting the new gentleman friend she took up with in her sixties. When I asked if she would marry him, she said, "I don't think so. You know they all come with the same pile of dirty laundry."

Now I understand what she meant. You swap one life for another and very soon you face new worries, new problems and stresses. Though with luck you handle them better. I swapped gut-wrenching television network problems, where you never knew when a series would be cancelled and the crew laid off, for the nightmare of the wild boar that keep digging up the lawn around the farm. Both are destructive but only the former gives me sleepless nights.

Your new life will not be paradise all the time. It would be strange if it was. There will be challenging days, boring days and days when you have to wonder if you did the right thing. But bit by bit your new chapter will become home.

That's how my next chapter worked out for me. I feel that I am the poster child for dreaming big, working hard and living with the consequences. I am so

thrilled by it all—despite the bumps along the way—
that I've written a book hoping to help you find a way.
When I mention to people that I live in Tuscany now,
I see the allure of my particular new chapter reflected
in their faces. They often smile and say, "You are living
my dream."

There is an astonishing dissimilarity between the
worlds I have lived in. I was born and raised in England,
spent my child-rearing years in Canada and for decades
worked in both the United States and Canada. I have
a condo in Toronto and a tiny house in London. And
now there is my new life in Italy. I am completely fascinated by this triangle of worlds, whose differences
can be so striking.

I often meet expats who have swapped their fascination with material wealth for the richness and rewards
of daily life in Italy and other places around the world.
My brother, Will, packed up his family (his second wife
and young daughter) and left behind the hectic pace of
New York City for the tranquility of Bali. He had worked
at a high level in advertising all his life, for very big
brands (Apple, Facebook, Coke and Toyota, to name just
a few). But he found himself at a point where the ad
world, and what it valued, just felt out of sync with what
he felt people need for themselves. He says, "Knowing
what we all stand for in life has become more and more
complicated. We have moved from a place where we
were already bombarded with product and service pro-
motions to a place of mass confusion where we're
inundated by millions upon millions of social compari-
sons. Tweets, pins, posts, snaps, blogs . . ."

Will realized he was exhausted with the status quo, and that he was not alone. His new chapter meant taking a walk from the industry he knew so well to begin something completely different in Bali—Elevation Barn, where he holds retreats utilizing the knowledge from his years in advertising to guide others as to how to work and play for a higher purpose rather than higher profits. His little girl now attends the Green School, an educational institution with a holistic approach to teaching conducted in a natural environment free of walls. When I asked him if there was anything he missed now that he has launched a new life in paradise, he said, "I do miss the pulse of New York but nothing outweighs the joy I see in my family's faces every day here in Bali. And I am loving connecting with myself, which allows me to step back and see the bigger picture. If I am to inspire others, it's imperative that I should be in the right mindset."

The whys, hows and whens of the decisions of everyone I have interviewed intrigue me, and luckily most are happy to share their stories. I found we all had the same goal in making the radical move: to bring balance back into our lives, to smile more and to find more joy in daily living.

My commute to the grocery store from my home just outside the thirteenth-century village walls of Montefollonico, is stunning, which makes this most mundane of chores a pleasure. The road takes me through postcard views of fields of wheat, vineyards and olive groves, and I always look for one particular field up on a hill that is carpeted with flowers in an array of colours like a Matisse painting. Since Italians tend to avoid growing anything they can't eat, a massive field of flowers really stands out.

One day my curiosity got the better of me and I turned off the main *strada* and onto a gravel road I hoped would lead me to the field. At the end of the road I found another story of next chapters. When I pulled up and parked by an ancient farm building surrounded by endless beds of glorious wild flowers, a beautiful young woman who looked like she was part of one of those paintings came towards me through the blossoms. When I asked her what they did on this farm, Mara invited me to join her and her two sisters for a glass of wine and a chat, as is the Italian way.

It turned out that Mara, Teresa and Laura had grown up on this property with their parents, who were sheep farmers. Mara left the farm to become a lighting director for a theatre company; Teresa became a garden designer and Laura went into the graphic arts. They worked in different cities in their own professions, but they always felt drawn back to the kind of life they led as children on the family farm—though they knew they didn't want to be sheep farmers!

In their thirties, all three women decided they couldn't ignore the pull any longer. They wanted to build new lives for themselves in their childhood home. What could they do? They had no clue. It turned out their mother held the key. She presented them with a book on flowers she thought they should read; before long they decided to grow and sell wild flowers. They already had the land, Teresa the garden designer knew plants, and the farm happened to be in an area of Tuscany where people came from around the world to marry or to celebrate important birthdays and anniversaries. The idea was also on trend. Many brides preferred the relaxed bohemian style and the romance of wildflowers, and wished for less formal bouquets and floral arrangements.

So their plan was a good one. They were not afraid of getting their hands dirty. What they did not have was money. So they roped in friends and families to build the beds and a few potting sheds, and help them with the plantings. Nature (and careful nuture) did the rest.

The next stumbling block came when they approached restaurants in the area to see if they would order their flowers. Italian proprietors did not see the point of decorating their tables with wild flowers, but several restaurants run by Americans shared their vision—the sisters were in business. Weddings and events soon followed. And when I feel the need for wild flowers, I now know where to go.

Tuscany is synonymous with the simple life, and that uncomplicated daily life is what drew me and my family to these hills. There are times, of course, usually as the long, summer months come to an end, when I have a craving for the city—for the streets of London, Toronto, New York. A yearning for a place with a structure, order and pace I totally understand. In Italy, the senses are never quiet. Even when I'm lying on a hammock reading a book, I find I'm listening to and watching the surrounding world. There are constant distractions: a coffee shop in the piazza begging me to take a seat, scents of a nonna's cooking spilling out of a local trattoria urging me to come taste, an undiscovered path luring me to wander down it or just sit and take in the view.

When I head home to Toronto or London, I am on a mission. I have things to do, meetings to take, friends to see. I assign each their allotted time and tick off every one. This can be quite reassuring and relaxing in its own way because I so completely understand this timetabled existence. In the *campagna*, we move to a different rhythm, and I had to climb a new learning curve in order to sink into it.

The historic villages and towns that surround me are quiet. They were designed for donkey carts, not cars. There are several advantages to the lack of vehicles in many of these places. We walk more, children still play in the streets, doors are rarely locked and neighbours look out for each other. Everyone knows everyone and they all know one another's business. I have ceased being surprised when I mention to the lady in the butcher's that I am returning to Canada next week and she replies that she already knows. Of course she does! But, along with what my old self might have regarded as *over*-familiarity comes a sense of comfort that is immeasurable.

As soon as Hans and I step out of the car after the long trip back to Italy, we each give a big sigh of relief. We are in our Italian home again. When I am not holding retreats, our days consist of trips to nearby towns, shopping at the weekly market and tackling new projects with the talented craftspeople who are fearless in the face of my wild ideas. I spend days sipping cappuccino in the piazza while gossiping with the villagers. I work in the lush vegetable garden that feeds us throughout the year. I spend hours just staring at the forever-changing view over the valley from my battered desk on the ancient stone terrace that has become my office *al fresco*.

Life here is about sharing uncomplicated stories, wrapped in summer warmth at the end of the day, about where to find a particular tractor part or when to start pruning the olive trees this year. It is a lunch that lasts for hours on mismatched chairs pulled up to a table strewn with local dishes and jugs of the rough (but now drinkable) wine from our own vineyard. The afternoon sun lulls us into siesta time and another list of chores is forgotten.

If anyone had told me when I was in my twenties that this would be my life I would have been horrified. In my thirties and forties, I would have been bewildered and unbelieving. Today, the life I once thought would only be a dream is my regular routine.

So are we living in Utopia? No, not at all. The same struggles and upsets that plague us all are still with me, but here in Tuscany the edges are softer and the core sweeter. I've had to remind myself at times that I am not on holiday in this tranquil landscape—I am *working*. The retreats take up a good portion of our year. They are lively and inspirational, but they are also hard work. Something always goes wrong.

I remember the very first evening of the first retreat we held at our own villa (after the golden moment of tears when the women all arrived). Hans was standing in front of the new, shiny, state-of-the-art electrical system that looked to me like a NASA flight deck. Holding his breath, he waited while eighteen women turned on their hairdryers at the same time as they spruced up for the evening. The system rose to the occasion, then conked out over dinner. What can I say? Candlelight is always more charming.

There are still moments when I question myself. Sometimes my new life in Tuscany can feel as if I have just moved offices. The work piles up just the same. There is a constant stream of colleagues asking questions. Back in Canada, a staffer might say, "We're off to Staples—do you want more writing pads?" Here, Evelina, my beloved housekeeper, wants to know why I have organized a picnic for the guests in the vineyard—is it okay for her to drive the food baskets up there on the tractor? Instead of disasters like the time when an entire shipment of my linens arrived in the stores and was of such poor quality we had to send it all back (at great expense!), I now face challenges like how to deal with a bug in the olive grove that means there will be no olive oil this year.

At my old house in Montreal, I complained about the invasion of squirrels that attacked the garbage and the destructive capabilities of the raccoon family in the attic. In Tuscany, we are in a nightly battle with herds of the notorious wild boar. The deer are so tame they wander through the courtyards devouring mouthfuls of lavender and ruining my beds. There always seems to be a bug of the month to freak us out. As I was proudly showing one woman her suite, she asked me if there were any nasty insects in Tuscany. Right beside my foot was a large black scorpion that I managed to finish off without her noticing while I was explaining how few bugs we get in this part of the world. Then, just before I left her room, a two-foot-long grass snake slithered from under the bed. This she saw and nearly headed back to the airport. It turned out to be nothing another glass of Prosecco couldn't fix.

Living in Tuscany has taught me that there is only so much you can control. I know it's a little corny, but what will be will be. Here, when we have had a hectic day, we pop over to the café in our village knowing we'll receive a warm welcome and an *aperitivo*. We walk home through our woods and chatter about sweet nothing. We pick some turnip leaves from the garden for dinner (in Tuscany they think turnips are all about the greens not the root!) and cook them in our own olive oil alongside a fried egg from our own chickens, whose yolk is the colour of a Tuscan sunset. There is always a story to tell about the day that makes us smile and smile we do, a lot. And pinch ourselves, because we have dreamt it, done it, and now we are living it, with all the consequences.

IT'S TIME TO TURN THE PAGE

I began this book by warning you that I am seriously unqualified to instruct anyone on anything. With only a high-school education and no letters after my name, all I can offer is my personal story and the know-how I've gained through pursuing my own next chapters. You can feel lonely when you set off on a new journey, but through my research into people who'd changed their lives, I've encountered countless kindred spirits. I am humbled and empowered by the hundreds of stories I have heard—and by the ones I have shared with you here. I have chatted over long-distance phone lines, shared steaming mugs of coffee in local cafés, emailed back and forth, and even become friends with some of the incredible, brave and inspirational souls I interviewed. They have all walked the walk, and then talked the talk with me honestly, and almost always with a big sense of humour.

Some of their stories are simple and others are extraordinary, but all the next chapters they shared took courage and perseverance. They are a diverse group, but each one found the wisdom to step out of their comfort zone and follow their dream.

You may have bought this book on a whim, or something inside you just made you pick it up. Maybe you've read it because you know you can't stand another day stuck doing the same old, same old.

But you know you need to design your next chapter if you find yourself thinking:

- My job is boring and going nowhere. It is time to turn the page.

- Life was full of purpose while I was raising my family, but now my children are gone. I need something to fill the void. It is time to turn the page.

- Retirement is dull. I could live another thirty years, and that's too long to be bored. It is time to turn the page.

- I've been successful in my field, but I've reached the end of the learning curve. It is time to turn the page.

- I survived an illness, and in the aftermath, I found a new zest for life and a big desire for change. It is time to turn the page.

- I've put in enough years working for someone else. Now I want to be my own boss. It is time to turn the page.

- Life has been good to me, but is this all there is to living? What about the welfare of others? It is time to turn the page.

If any of these statements describes you, turn that page and:

1. **Find your passion!**
   Dig deep, travel, explore and play until you unearth your joy.

2. **Do your research!**
   Check out everything you need to learn before you start. Ask for help and advice wherever you can.

3. **Get connected!**
   Contact everyone from your past and present who can be a sounding board and give you guidance.

4.   **Get moving!**

Whether you are beginning big or small, just get going. Ignore all those excuses to stall. Disregard the naysayers. Keep your vision in focus and never let fear paralyze you into passivity.

5.   **Never be afraid to ask for advice!**

We are all learning, so always ask others you trust for help.

6.   **Use your strengths and skills!**

Your past experience is your greatest gift.

7.   **Confidence is crucial!**

Insecurity is normal. To pull this off you need to lose the self-doubt and respect your own capabilities.

8.   **Take risks!**

It is impossible to move forward without taking risks. Think hard about the level of risk that's right for you, financially or otherwise. Some risk in life is better than no risk at all.

9.   **Leap that wall!**

My brother, Will, always says when you hit an obstacle—which you will at some point—don't give up. Work on a way of going under, over or around it. There is always a way.

10. **Throw out the rule books!**

This is your next chapter and there is no right or wrong path to head down. Build an empire, make a fortune, or forget about all that and just do something you love.

And here we are at the end. Remember you are not alone in wanting to make change in your life. Walk on past that crossroads—the world is waiting for you. I am off to the pub now to toast us all!

xx Debbie

Letters to
Yourself

My Past

Letters to
Yourself

My Future

Letters to
Yourself

My Ideas

Letters to
Yourself

My Fears

Letters to
Yourself

My Excuses

Letters to Yourself

What
Brings
Me Joy

NEXT CHAPTERS

Alex's story — vintagerosecupcakes.com

Christine's story — whatshesaidtalk.com

Dieter and Cindy's story — maisonalergria.com

Frances' story — Francesmayesbooks.com

Helen's story — helenosheamusic.com

Joanna's story — knixwear.com

Kareen's story — artofabstraction.com

Lucy's story — nowteach.org.uk

Mara's story — puscinaflowers.com

Marni's story — marniwasserman.com

Natasha's story — hustleetheart.com

Nina's story — blackroosterdecor.com

Philip's story — rdjrecordings.com

Sharon's story — soupsisters.org

Sian's story — siantravis.com

Susan's story — wecare.com

Tricia's story — lookfabulousforever.com

Will's story — elevationbarn.com

———

Debbie Travis — Tuscangetaway.com

debbietravis.com

Lucy McInnes — lifeandsoulcoach.com

———

tefllife.com teaching abroad

globalworkandtravel.com

Worldteachers.com

Redcross.org.uk

Redcross.ca

ACKNOWLEDGEMENTS

Design Your Next Chapter is a deeply personal book. At times I found it difficult to share my feelings. Knowing how hard it was for me, I want to give an especially heartfelt thank you to all the courageous people who generously shared their dreams, their challenges and their own next chapters with me, and now with you. I wish each and every one of you happiness and success in your new ventures.

I am profoundly grateful to the entire team at Penguin Random House Canada. I am entirely indebted to the wisdom of my editor, Anne Collins, for her tireless hand-holding and her endless enthusiasm. Her brilliance in bringing order to my chaos is epic. Another huge thanks to the book's designer, Lisa Jager, for listening to my ideas and then creating such a beautiful and cheerful book. Thank you to Matthew Sibiga, Sarah Smith-Eivemark, Daniel French and the entire sales and marketing team for their confidence in me and for getting the message out there to all those who have found themselves at a crossroads and may find their new direction in these pages. I am sincerely grateful to Ann Jansen for her guidance on the audio book—what a fun experience. A big thanks, too, to Zoe Maslow, who helped me put together the proposal, and to Cathy Paine for always believing in me.

Throughout the book, I have pitched the merits of sharing ideas with the people you trust—and I drew heavily on the patience and support of my friends and family. They have listened to me for more hours than I can count as I read chapters out loud to them; the book has benefited enormously from their valuable comments. Thank you, thank you, thank you to Josh, Max, Fiona, Andrea, Jacky, Gaye and Helen. Thanks to Frances Mayes for writing her glorious book, *Under the Tuscan Sun*, which inspired me to leap into my own next chapter, and for many other things too. Thank you to Trish, who inspires so many, and especially me. A special thanks to Sian, my sister-in-law. She bravely shared with me all her worries and fears about facing the empty nest so those who find themselves in the same place would feel less alone.

I often drew on the wisdom and judgment of my good friend, Lucy McInnes, a talented life coach and patient listener. Thank you, Lucy, for your advice. My gratitude, always, to Jacky and Steve, who have been a key part of my own next chapter since day one and are now embarking on their own. A heartfelt thanks to the many other people who have given me their love and support while I wrote.

My love and thanks go to my two precious sons and their beautiful girlfriends, who have listened to my dreams for so many years. They are my pride and joy and they teach me daily how to be a better mother. Finally, I would like to thank Hans. No man should ever put up with what he has gone through while I demanded solitude and quiet places to write. His patience and kindness is never-ending. And, dear Hans, I pray it never does end.

DEBBIE TRAVIS is an international television icon, a bestselling author, a newspaper columnist, a sought-after public speaker and the centre of a small business empire. Her shows, *Debbie Travis' Painted House*, *Debbie Travis' Facelift*, *From The Ground Up* and *All for One*—and most recently the six-part documentary, *La Dolce Debbie*, about how she transformed a thirteenth-century Tuscan farmhouse into a hotel and retreat—have been seen in Canada, the United States and eighty other countries. She has authored nine previous books (eight on decorating); Oprah has called her "the master of paint and plaster." Having stepped back from TV producing, she gets to relax, just a little, running a luxury boutique hotel where like-minded women can experience the Tuscan lifestyle at her Girls' Getaways, and a one-hundred-acre farm where she produces an organic Extra Virgin Olive Oil and a variety of lavender products. Debbie shares her journey with her husband, Hans, and two sons, Josh and Max.